SCRATCH C[...]
FOR K[...]

Have Fun with Computer Coding, Creating Awesome Projects, Animations And Simulations. With this Guide You Will be Able to Create Your Games in Few Days and Master Scratch.

CHRISTIAN MORRISON

TABLE OF CONTENTS

INTRODUCTION

What is Programming

Programming is a good and useful skill, which every child should learn. In later years, this skill may be used to create and develop great things. These things may be intended for entertainment during the childhood and teenage years. But, many of these things raise an interest in programming that can later be a solid basis for a career in computer science, engineering, or some other computer-related profession. These professions today are very popular among young people. Programming basics are something that anyone who will one day work with computers should have a good grasp of.

There are so many different programming languages, intended for creating different sorts of programs. The general rule is that any language can be used to make any kind of program. But, is it true? We will discover the answer to this question in this book. Some of these programming languages can be hard to learn, while others are as simple as the alphabet we learned as small children. It is entirely up to you to decide which one will be the best to pick for your students. Just keep in mind that every person (and this applies to children also) is an individual. Not all of us have the same interests, so consider allowing them input when it comes to deciding which of the programming languages, they like best. You should present them with a few, for example Ruby, Python, and Java, explain to them what the advantages and disadvantages are for each of them. Then, to keep it interesting, you might give them examples of programs and platforms they are familiar with and explain to them which programming language are they based on. For example, if you tell a child who has an account on Twitter that this social network was built using the Ruby programming language, they may become interested in learning more about Ruby, because this language is what made their favorite pastime possible. By learning about the programming languages that made their favorite games, applications and social networks possible, they will also learn how to behave safely when it comes to computers and data they post on the Internet. So, this is another good thing that will come out of the first coding course.

What is Syntax?

Computers are machines and, as such, they understand only what we type if we type it in the exact manner that the computer expects you to. This is a basic must if you want your machine to work properly and to give you your desired results. The expected way of writing in a computer program is called syntax. This means that syntax represents a set of rules in spelling and grammar both when using programs and also when creating them. This is, in other words, the grammar of programming. Without the knowledge and correct use of syntax, we cannot use any program, much less make one.

Programming syntax contains strings similar to words, somewhat similar to a human language we use in our everyday lives. Correctly formed syntax strings or lines result in syntactically correct sentences within a specific programming language, in the same way that correct sequencing and use of letters when you write them down form a word and correct sequencing of words make a meaningful sentence. When we're talking syntax, what we are referring to is a collection of rules governing the structure of the language. You'll find that syntax rules are unavoidable in programming, as not following the syntax of a language results in your program failing to run. In the first case, the document is treated as source code, while in another case, the document is essentially a set of data to be processed.

Lower-level computer programming languages are rooted in distinct sequences of symbols. There are also some higher-level programming languages, which often have visuals, which may be denoted by either text or a graphical interpretation. Syntactically invalid documents are said to have a syntax error. That means, for example, if we type an incorrect code or command, the program will send us a notification that a syntax error occurred and that, with an incorrect command, we cannot proceed without correcting that error--an error that could be as simple as an overlooked typo.

Syntax is divided into three equally important parts: phrases, context and individual words.

Words represent the so-called "lexical level," determining how characters form pieces of a line in a code, or the whole code;

Phrases, or the so-called "grammar level," narrowly speaking, have the function of determining and distinguishing parts of the code from phrases;

Context represents a function that is determining to which objects or variables certain names refer to, if their types are valid, etc.

Distinguishing between these differences in this way allows us process each level individually, rather than having to load up everything every time you start up the application.

Why is syntax so important in programming?

Without syntax, no programming languages can exist. It is as if you have a language but no letters.

It would mean that we can speak in that language, but we have no way of writing our thoughts on it. That kind of language would not have any sense and would serve little useful purpose. Some of the factors related to the syntax of a programming language are readability, writability, and program expectations. In most cases, regardless of what their opinion is on a particular syntax, programmers use any available syntax and enjoy trying different things. Nevertheless, we have to ask and answer two simple syntax-related questions: Why is syntax so important in programming? Can syntax be easily changed?

The answer to the first question would be that the syntax is important because it is directly related to many factors of programming. Some of these factors are readability, writability, and program expectations. It is the grammar of a computer program, after all, the very backbone of the code. In most cases, you will like a given syntax or you will dislike it, but some programs may use any syntax and in so doing, you will enjoy trying different things and seeing what works best for you and for the children in your life.

As for the second question, my opinion is that we have to learn the syntax before we get the idea of changing it. If we do not know the syntax well enough (or we do not know the syntax at all, in some cases, as with beginners) we cannot know whether it suits us. Before you aim to change something, you should get to know the thing (in this case, a language) you wish to change. However, being able to change the syntax of a given programming language depends on the design and implementation of the language. For example, in the programming language that is called the Ring, the syntax can be changed very easily. For the other programming languages this varies from language to language. Basically, they all have their settings and syntax rules. Knowledge of the syntax rules of every programming language is essential for their adequate and successful use in coding or programming. But before getting any ideas about changing the syntax, we have to consider how the codes are written. We should also have in mind what a particular function or syntax rule enables us to do.

One important thing to note is that you can (most often during the run-time) change the language's keywords as many times as you want to and you can create different, custom styles for your source code. Creating a custom style (or changing the language keywords) can be useful in many ways. Let's explore a few examples to bring this into context:

This includes language translation from English keywords to Arabic, French, etc. Most uses of this function are applied in translating programs and applications that allow you to translate a given text from one language to another.

Easy storage and updates needed for some of your old codes (in old programming languages used at the time when the particular program was made). This also means that you may not only store but also use the programs written in older programming languages. The only condition here is that the programs stored must be updated.

Freedom for different teams working on different subsystems in the project, where each team can use their favorite style, is also very important for any given programming language. Besides that, if more than one team is working on one project, they can function and work separately. That means that no team may interfere with the work of another.

Syntax changes are good for research and trying different styles before choosing the syntax usage best suited to your programming needs. This has an enormous practical value, since that way, we can test our changes in simple things and programs, before trying them with more serious and demanding programs, languages and/or projects. It is also a great way to learn and to test our abilities, which is highly valuable for both adults and children alike. Besides proving ourselves as good programmers, it is also a way to design something new and unique, something we can call our own. Just be careful. You might end up with something more complicated than you intended. However, even this can be a great opportunity for growth as a programmer. Changes, in general, are a good thing because there is always a chance to create something better.

Where do we start?

When writing about the syntax of a programming language, the big question is: Where do we start? Do we start within explaining what the syntax of a computer programming language is, how we use it and what we need it for, as well as their practical application, or do we start somewhere else? What is the simplest answer to the question of what syntax is and what the importance of syntax is for us?

Syntax can be described as a kind of bridge between the machine and you. You and your computer are connected by the syntax your computer needs you to enter in order for it to execute your commands. If the syntax is wrong, the computer is unable to follow up and execute any given tasks or commands. It "does not understand" (let me put it this way) what you are telling it to do, because you have "told" (a better term here might be "written," since we write our codes) it in the wrong way - you have used the wrong syntax, or, you have used the correct syntax, but in the wrong way.

CHAPTER - 1

GETTING STARTED WITH SCRATCH

What is Scratch?

Scratch is a graphic programming environment developed by a group of researchers from the Lifelong Kindergarten Group of the MIT Media Laboratory, under the direction of Dr. Mitchel Resnick.

This graphic environment makes programming more attractive and accessible for anyone who faces for the first time to learn a programming language. According to its creators, it was designed as a means of expression to help children and young people express their ideas creatively while developing logical thinking skills.

Scratch allows you to easily create your own interactive stories, animations, games, record sounds and make artistic creations.

The application of block programming languages allows a visual presentation of the paradigm and methodology of computer programming allowing to focus on the logic of programming leaving aside the syntax of programming languages (semicolons, parentheses, etc.).

Scratch, The Programming Language

It is a visual programming language, oriented to the teaching of block programming to children, without having to delve deeply into the development of the code.

It is a project created by MIT, launched in 2005, free and open-source; available for Windows, Mac, and Linux.

Scratching is an English term that means reusing code, and that means that the program allows you to use internal resources and modify them to the user's liking.

Characteristics and virtues

- You can handle it online or offline. The good thing about the first is that it is always updated, making the user experience never stop improving. Here you can download the software, in case you want to use it on a computer without an Internet connection.

- The Scratch programming language works with blocks, where the user places some bricks with certain conditions, which make the object move to one side or the other.

- It is a collaborative environment, where each user can participate in several projects, moving blocks and interacting with the object.

- Those same blocks are classified by colors, making operation even more intuitive.

- Based on the Logo programming language, developed by Danny Bobrow, among others.

- It is usually recommended for children between 6 and 16 years old, but as we said, it can be used by anyone who wants, without any type of cutter.

- Programs can be launched directly from a web page.

- Autonomous Learning.

- Benefits of this programming language:

- Free, free software.

- Ideal for taking the first steps in the world of code.

- Available in several formats: offline (download on Windows, Mac, and Linux), and online.

- Once the project is finished, it can be downloaded and shared on the internet.

- You can use it in many languages.

- With the Scratch programming language, you learn to program without typing code.

- Transmits to the child the need to solve problems in an orderly manner.

- Being a scalable learning method, a problem can always be further developed, increasing the level of the challenge, and consequently, expanding the creative ability of the student.

- Depth of mathematical concepts: coordinates, algorithms, variables, or randomness, among others.

- Develop the capacity of self-criticism, doubting any hypothetical solution.

Scratch, The Code Editor

The Scratch editor divides the screen into several panels: on the left are the stage and the list of objects, in the middle are the block palettes and on the right the program, costumes and sounds editor. The block palette contains a series of blocks that can be dragged and dropped in the Programs area to build the scripts that constitute our project. The block palette is divided into ten groups of blocks: Motion, Appearance, Sound, Pencil, Data, Events, Control, Sensors, Operators, and More Blocks (to create special blocks and other extensions).

Let's go by parts!

- Contents

- The objects

- Information about an Object

- The costumes

- The sounds

- The programs

- The blocks

- Stage

- Top bar

The Objects

The Objects area can manage the objects or characters that we have been adding to the program. We can select the object we want to edit or add a new object:

Both from the gallery of Scratch characters, and drawing a new one, uploading a photo that we have on our computer or taking a photo if we have a webcam installed:

Information about an Object

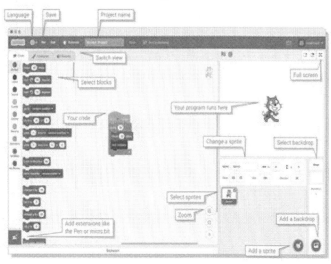

By clicking on the blue i in the upper corner of the object we can access the information panel of that object being able to edit among other things the name of the object.

The costumes

In the area of costumes we can add or draw different images for our characters as well as edit them. With the program we can control with what costume the character will be shown on stage.

The sounds

It allows you to add or edit sounds to our characters, both from the Scratch sound gallery and from files that we have on our computer.

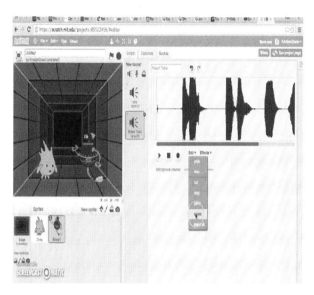

The programs

The Programs tab contains the instruction blocks assembled so that they give life to our object.

From the block area you can drag and drop the different blocks to the Programs area where they can be assembled together forming the programs of our project.

Each of the objects in the Object area, including the scenario, has its own programs that control only that particular object.

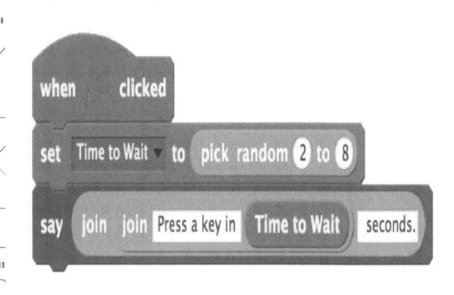

The blocks

The block palette contains a series of blocks that can be dragged and dropped in the Programs area to build the scripts that constitute our project. The block palette is divided into ten groups of blocks: Motion, Appearance, Sound, Pencil, Data, Events, Control, Sensors, Operators, and More Blocks (to create special blocks and other extensions).

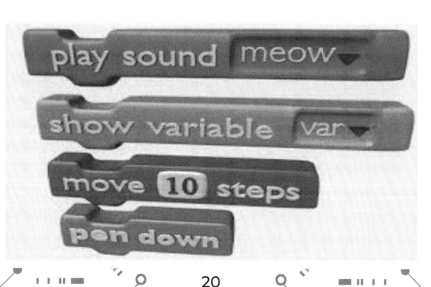

Stage

The scenario is a type of object that represents the background of the screen and is the place where all other objects interact.

As an object: that Programs, Costumes and Sounds can be added in a similar way to other objects.

As a place: where the rest of the objects interact, it represents a coordinate system where the center would be the point 0.0 (x = 0, y = 0) where the x correspond to the horizontal position and the y to the vertical position.

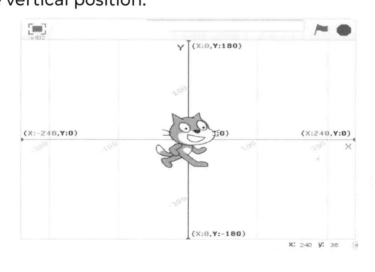

Top bar

Scratch button

Allows you to exit and return to the main page of the Scratch website

Menu file

New: Create a new blank project.

Save now: save the project in its current state

Save a copy: Create a copy of the current project to modify it.

Go to My Stuff: Link to the My Stuff section, where all your projects are.

Upload from your computer: Upload .sb2 projects you have saved.

Download to your computer: download the current project in .sb2 format

Revert: returns the project to its initial state before opening it the last time.

Edit menu

Undelete – Its function is to undo a sprite, costume, sound, or script that was recently deleted.

Small stage layout – Its funtion is to make the stage shrink to a s not a big size, i.e., a maller size.

Turbo Mode – It is where the code is executed very quickly. It is for setting the player into Turbo Mode.

Edit Buttons

Below you can find 4 buttons with which you can edit the Objects or Programs.

Duplicate: allows you to create a copy of the object or program we stamp

Cut: allows you to cut and eliminate the object or program in which we put the scissors.

Expand: allows you to enlarge the size of an object on the stage

Reduce: allows you to reduce the size of an object on the stage

Help: open the description, in English, of a block in the help section.

Building & Running a Script

As far as, Scratch will run one block from every script each tick. Let's say you had these scripts:

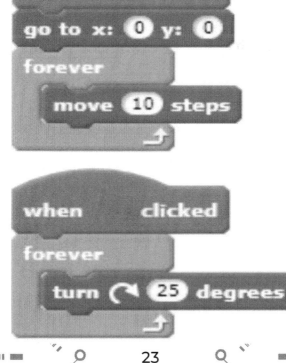

As soon as you click the green flag, the program will run the first block of the first script (go to 0, 0). Scratch will find the next running script (the second one) and run the first block there. So, loops such as forever and repeat count as blocks, so nothing would happen, except that the loop would start.

What scratch is going to do is to go back to the first script and check the next block (forever) and run that (again doing nothing). So, it will move to the next running script and run the other block, the next, in this case, in line (turn 25 degrees).

Look that, it will jump back to first script and move 10 steps, then go to script 2 and turn 25 degrees. And, there will be a continuity of alternative between moving and turning for the rest of the project.

The tricky part is that the order in which scripts are run (which is run first, the one with the moving block or the turn block?) is difficult to pin down. Keep in mind that, in scratch, it's up to you to place scripts wherever you would like them go first. That means, basically, the scripts run from the top to the bottom, with no concern for their x location.

So, one more time, the complications of the things get worse. You have to know which sprite you will fire first when there are multiple sprites involved.

Important: Make sure to not confuse sin the custom blocks with "run without screen refresh" checked are treated as just one block in the execution order.

Fortunately, the users who program in this way (rather than using, for example, broadcasts) are generally making projects simple enough that it doesn't matter the order in which events are fired.

Creating a Scratch account

Download and install directly from the project website: http://scratch.mit.edu/

In the zone "Download Scratch" we can find an installer for Windows and Mac. There are not yet specific packages for Linux (they indicate that they are working on it), but there are some instructions on how to make it work under different distributions of this system in the project forums.

In the first execution of the program, the environment is in English:

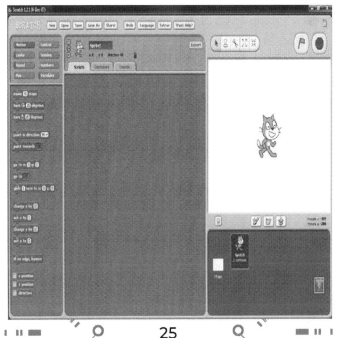

For switching the language, you just need to make a click on the "Language" button. Select "the language you want"...

Scratch Installation

To download the latest version, go to http://scratch.mit.edu/ and follow the download link. After clicking the download link, this page will pop to your screen:

If you don't have Adobe AIR, you have to click and download it. Just follow the instructions to install it. After installing Adobe Air, click Scratch offline Editor Download depending on your OS.

After downloading the file, click the .exe file from the bottom left of your screen.

Click run to install Scratch to your PC.

Wait the setup to finish.

After the initial installation, click continue.

Click I Agree.

Wait for the installation to finish.

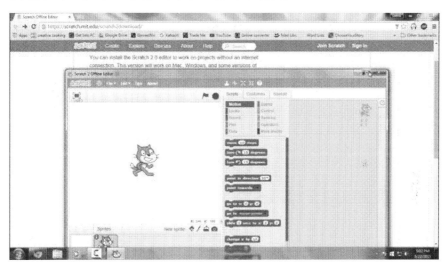

And your done!

CHAPTER - 2
THE BASIC OF SCRATCH

Variables

In Scratch programming, Variables are used to store values. We have already been using some variables in creating our project. For example, in the Up and Down project, we made use of the to check if the sprite was near the edge. In the project after this, we also used the and to change the position of the Sprite 1 to Sprite 2.

All these three palettes are examples of the variable used in Scratch programming. Scratch stores values in these variables; these values are what we use in creating our programs.

We also recall that in some of our project, we altered the values of some variables to fit into what we want. As much as Scratch already has its own variables, we can create our own variables and use this to keep value. A good example of a variable palette that can be altered is the more () block. We can use variables to keep the score of a game, to store speed and to determine the value of x and y in equations.

The two types of variables that would be considered:

- Numerical Variables
- String Variables

Numerical Variables

1. Project name: Times 2

2. Start a new project and title it Times 2

3. Go to the Data block and click on Make a Variable. Title the variable Number and select for this sprite only, then select the OK option

NB: You can share variables among all the sprites or use it with only one sprite. This type of variable can only be used to determine the position of x in a particular sprite. While is an example of a variable that can be used by any sprite. Local variables are variables you can use with only one sprite, while global variables are variables that use all of the sprites.

4. Run your program, when it starts running, go to the Sensing block and use the ask _____ and wait to ask for a number

5. Scratch keeps all the numbers you enter in the answer variable from the Sensing menu. Go to Go Data menu, open set _____ to ____ block. Use this to keep the answers to the variables in the number

variables. Below is how to achieve this:

- Create a local variable and name it Plus 2. After this, go to the Operator block, use the +operator to store the local variable created in the sum of number + 2

- Go to the Looks block, open the way ____ for 2 secs block to view the number + 2 score.

- Start your program, put in a number, and then confirm if it is showing the right answer.

- Make local variables to maintain the value of the number minus two and times two, determine these variables, and show their values. (We will observe that the multiplication operation makes use of an asterisk. This is so because, in programming, letter x is usually used as a variable. Using it again as a multiplication sign would be confusing).

- Test run your program to confirm it is showing the right answer.

It is noteworthy that this program cannot be written without variables because you are not aware of the number the user would choose, hence there is no way you would compute the value of the number without the use of variables.

String Variables

Name of Program: additional 2 (continued)

The user's number minus, times, and plus two were displayed. It would make sense to leave the user more informed. For example: making the number plus 2 = 7

Steps to adding more information to the variable

1. Start a new local variable called output.

2. Then put the plus2 variable to number + 2, after this determine the output variable by using the join operator in the Operators menu

3. Switch your 'say plus2' for 2 secs block so you can use the output variable.

4. Start your program and confirm it is working well.

5. Adapt your program to enable it to use the output variable to show the numerical values of 2 and times 2.

Algorithms

In Scratch programming, algorithms are a set of instructions that are used to complete a task. This task could be something unseen, like tracking the breakout of a dead and rotten dog through the air. However, whether seen or unseen, it is advisable to think of the algorithm you would be using before starting your program. A good example of the algorithm for graph is y = 4x +8. We will be creating a program and use algorithms for the program.

Program name: Sum of the Numbers 1 to n

Assuming you were asked a very simple question like, "What is the total number of 1 to 3?" This is quite easy; you would only calculate 1+2+3=6. The estimate of 1to 3 is 6. What if the question is 1to 7, you would calculate 1+2+3+4+5+6+7= 28? But if the question is 1 to 60? This is quite technical, to solve this, let's go into programming

1. Start a new project and title it Numbers 1 to n

2. Generate three local variables, title them Number, Summation and EndValue respectively

3. Initiate 3 as EndValue

4. Initiate the local variable Number to 1 and Summation to 0

5. Add the following repeat loops to your script:

   • In the first loop iteration, the number (1) result derived is still less than the EndValue (3) we are aiming at. As a result, we keep running the iteration

   • When the first block in the loop is iterated, the new total value is set to (0) plus number (1). This makes the overall value 0 + 1 = 1.

However, since the answer we are aiming at is number (3), we run another interaction with the second block in the loop. Our new value when the second block add 1 to the previous result is 1 + 1 =

2. After the second iteration, the result is still less than the required EndValue (3). We go inside again to carry out another iteration until we arrived at the desired number (3)

- Add blocks to display the output using the string "The sum of the numbers from 1 to n is: m", where n is the number we entered at the beginning of the program, and m is the Sum.

- Run your program to test what you have just done.

NB: The act of changing the value of a fixed amount is very common in loops. This process is called incrementing the variable.

Summation of the Even/Odd Numbers 1 to n

You find the sum of the even/odd number 1 to n; we would be creating a new program with the name " Sum 1 to n Even/Odd."

- Use the same method in the above program to write a program

- Request a number from the user and show the summation of all the odd numbers from 1 to n, and the summation of the even numbers from 2 to n. For instance, if the user puts in 6, the display would be 9 (that is 1 + 3 + 5) and 12 (that is 2 + 4 + 6).

Program Structure

Virtually all the programs that have been created so far are single script programs. Complex script programs are created with more than one script. Although single script programs seem easier, when a single script program becomes too long, any of these two problems can occur.

- Poor reading proficiency. The cluster of details in a single script program sometimes makes it too clumsy to read. It is easier to get lost while going through the clumps of details in the single script.

- The program becomes difficult to manage. The length of the program often causes this problem. To control the program Arranging length, the programmer would have to arrange and modify the program script. Doing this is always very difficult because each detail contains in the script of the program. This problem made it difficult to reuse parts of the script in creating another script.

We will examine how to use messages and more blocks to add structure to a program and how this structuring can be used to control the length of the script. Below are the steps to adding more blocks to a script.

1. Create a single script program and make the script do the following actions:

2. Open on the left side.

3. Move 10 steps at a time, making a total of 200 steps.

4. Jump up 25 steps (and fall) 3 times.

5. Turn and take 100 steps back, making sure you take 10 steps each time.

6. Turn 2 times.

7. Spin and take 500 steps, making sure you take 10 steps each time.

Adding Structures with Messages

Let's assume the program we created can perform all the actions mentioned above effectively; the layout of the script will be piled up with different instructions. These instructions would make it difficult to keep track of the series of instructions clustered in the program because the single script program is a lengthy set of commands devoid of a solid structure. In computer programming, this type of structure is known as spaghetti code. Spaghetti code is not only difficult to read but also hard to rearrange (moving first and jumping second) and to change (adding a second group of five jumps).

To fix this, each set of actions — initialize, walk, jump, run — would be replaced with a message and another script. For example, we would adjust the loop to jump three times with this broadcast ___ and wait block and the when I receive ___ script

After this action, it would be observed that the blocks we used in adding the structure to the program are the broadcast ___ and wait block and not broadcast ___. This is because when we use a broadcast ___ block without the wait block, it passes control immediately to the next block without waiting for the scripts that received the message to finish the process. For instance, the message in the program above is for the sprite to jump and then spin:

The next final step we would take is the replace step. Go to the Broadcast-and-wait block, then initialize spin to two times, jump to 3 times, walk to 200 times, walk to 100 steps.

How to Add More Blocks to a Program

After the first process, the sprite would look a lot better and easier to work on. The only difficulty we would encounter is with the walk block repeated about three times. Although each walk block has a defined number of times that determines how far the sprite would walk, we will be redefining this with the More block. In Scratch programming, the More block is usually defined by the programmer. The block derives its name "More" from the fact that the programmer is the one to define or determine how it would operate. In programming, this process of adding a block to a program is known as Function.

CHAPTER - 3

FUNCTIONS, IF STATEMENT, AND LISTS

Why Use Functions?

When you used the repeat command, it made drawing complex shapes real y easy. Now you will learn about functions, which allow you to repeat the same code over and over again without having to rewrite the code. A function may sound an awful lot like the repeat command, but functions are one of the most useful tools a programmer can have because it allows you to adjust certain parts of the code based on your needs.

The limitation of the repeat command is apparent when you want to draw a bunch of different size squares. Each square will be coded with virtual y identical code

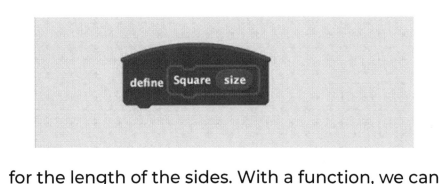

for the length of the sides. With a function, we can use one block of code to draw different size squares!

Formatting Functions have to be written in a particular way. A function must have a name and it may have zero or it may have multiple inputs.

Inputs Scratch offers three different types of inputs: number, string, and boolean. Strings are words like "hello" or

"program." Booleans can have only two values: true or false. Final y, numbers are values like 23.56 or 200.

Create a Function To create a function, go to the More Blocks section and click on the "Make a Block" button.

Then, enter a name for your function. If your function needs to use input values, click on one of the options and enter a name for the input.

Click to add the "size" input The input value

The function name

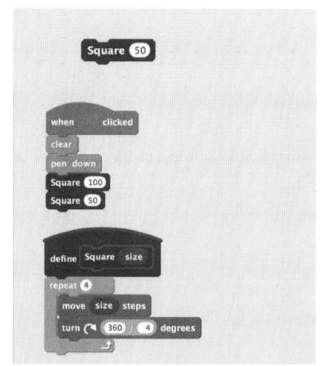

Calling A Function, you can make a script attached to a define block and click "run," but nothing will happen.

This is because you have to tell the computer to call the function. The way you call the "Square" function defined on the previous page is by using the following command block, which was created at the same time as the function.

In the example above, the input value is 50, but it could be set to any number.

Draw a square with a length of 100

Draw a square with a length of 50

Click and drag the "size" input to get a copy of "size." Then drop it in the placeholder for "move steps"

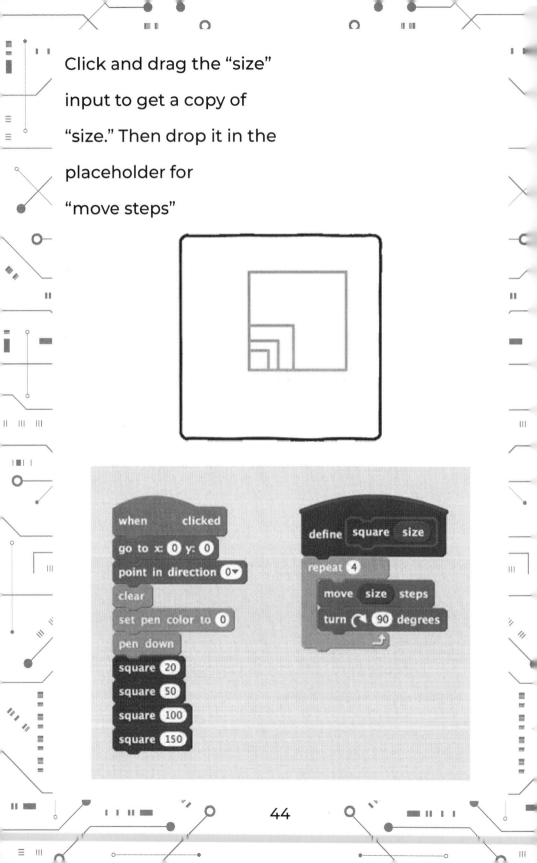

Project: Drawing Squares

Let's use a function to draw a bunch of different size squares. Can you draw some other size squares?

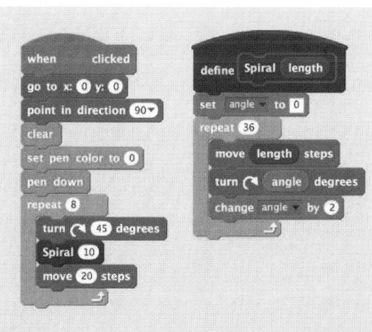

Project: Spiral Rose

You can combine repeats and functions to make the spiral rose to the left.

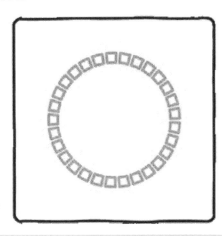

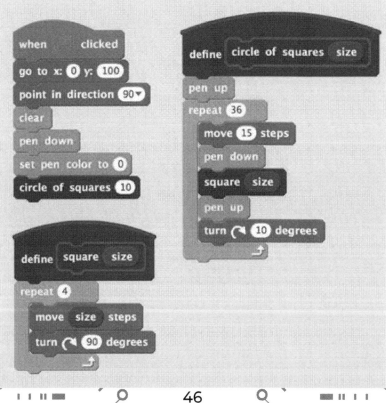

Project: Circle of Squares

You can make a lot of complicated things easily with

functions. In this function, the command penup is used to stop the pen from making marks while it is moving.

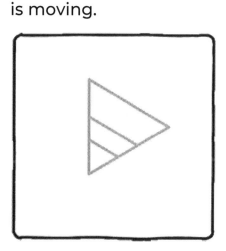

Ch 9: Practice Problems

1) Can you make a function that will help you draw different size triangles?

2) Make a function that will let you draw different size houses.

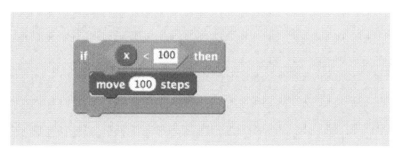

If Statements

What if you wanted your pen to do different things based on the current value of a variable? If the variable's value is greater than zero, the pen should rotate 45 degrees. If the variable's value is equal to zero, the pen should rotate 90 degrees. An easy way to program this is to use an if statement.

If Statement The if statement tells your program to execute a certain section of code only if a particular condition is true. If it is true, the code between the brackets will be executed. If it is false, Scratch will simply ignore the code between the brackets.

Compare "x" to 100

This code will only ex-

ecute if the value stored

in "x" is less than 100

Conditional Statements Scratch lets you compare values to see if one is greater than the other, less than the other, or equal to the other value.

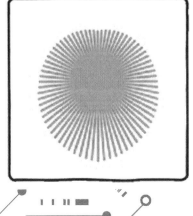

Conditional Statements

Command

Example

Command In Scratch

equal to

5 = 6

less than

10 < 3

greater than

8 > 5

Project: Radiating Lines

To make the image to the left, use two if statements to adjust the length of the lines.

The repeat command is going to run 73 times. You are going to use a variable called count to keep track of what number repeat we are on. If the count is less than 36, de-crease the line length. If the count is greater than 36, increase the line length.

You can use this technique to draw different shapes de-pending on your if statements. What will happen if you use four if statements instead of the two in the example?

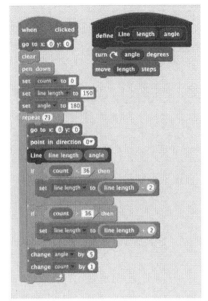

If the count is less than 36, decrease the line length
If the count is greater than 36, increase the line length

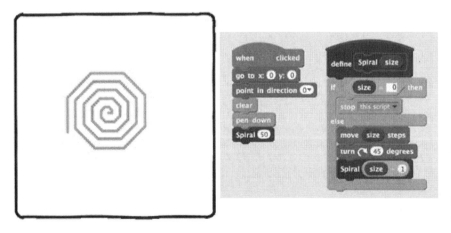

Project: Recursive Spiral

An interesting thing about functions are that they can call themselves. Whenever a function calls itself, it is called recursion. The only problem with this technique is that you need a way to stop the calling process or else the program will run forever!

If loops are helpful for stopping the program because you can tell the program to stop once a certain condition has been met. For example, you could initially call the loop with the variable "size" that has been initialized to 100. Each time the loop calls itself, the "size" decreases by 1. When the value of "size" reaches 0, the program will stop.

When size equals 0, stop the program

The Spiral function calls itself with size-1

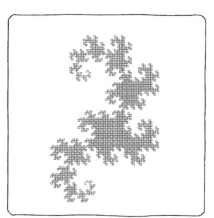

Project: Dragon Curve

Programmers like recursion a lot because it lets them make real y complicated drawings using relatively few lines of code. If you tried to draw the dragon curve above only by using functions and repeat loops, it would take you hours, and hundreds of lines of code, to complete.

Try experimenting with the code on the next page by calling the function with different inputs (for example call the function x with x 6 or x 13).

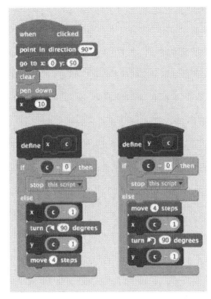

Try changing the input to a different number like 6 or 13

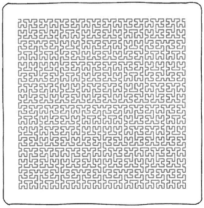

Project: Hilbert Curve

The labyrinth above is called the Hilbert curve. Like the dragon curve, it is real y easy to draw with a recursive function.

After you copy the code on the next page into

Scratch and run the program, try experimenting with altering the code. For instance, try changing the inputs for the lsec function call in the last line of code to lsec 5 5 or lsec 3 3.

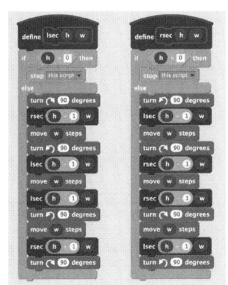

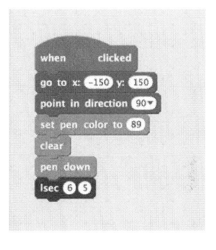

try changing the inputs to different numbers like (lsec 5 5) or (lsec 3 3) 53

Practice Problems

1) Can you make a recursive spiral triangle?

2) Use the spiral triangle code from above to make a star.

Experiment with different angles and lengths to create different types of stars.

Making Lists

So far, we have only used Scratch to manipulate numbers and variables one value at a time, but we can also store and manipulate lists of things.

Lists Remember when you learned about variables? Variables are a way to store one thing in memory. Sometimes you need to store multiple things in memory but you don't want to do a lot of tedious typing. Lists let you store many values in a single structure.

Making lists is like making a variable.

Go to the Data Section and click

the "Make List" button then enter the name of the list.

You can then use the add

block to add items to the list.

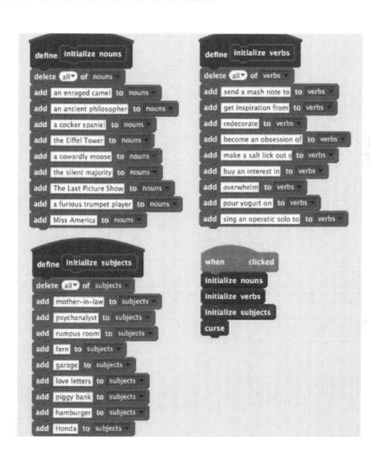

Project: Curses

This program is based on the work of Tom Dwyer and Margot Critchfield, who published a similar program in their book BASIC and the Personal

Computer in 1979. It uses lists to create a computer-generated poem.

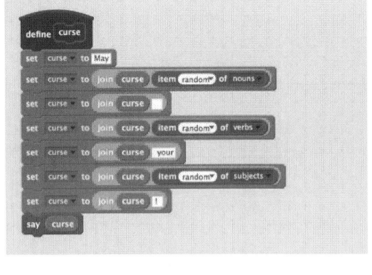

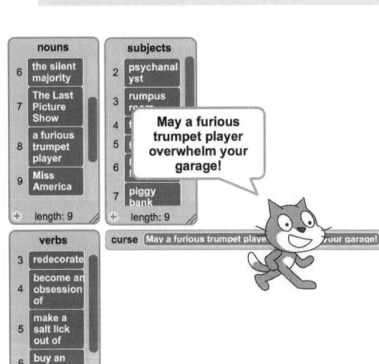

Change this program to suit your personality. Add more things to the lists. Take some things away. Change the pattern used to form the curse. Is the pattern for a blessing different from the pattern for a curse?

Practice Problems

1) Many computer programs have been developed that generate poetry or music. Some of them use a technique similar to the curses program. These programs often have large lists of words that are arranged according to some predefined patterns.

For example, you might draw from lists in a pattern like this:

Title

Adjective Noun

Verb Noun

Noun Preposition Noun Verb Noun

Ending Phrase

How could you make your poem rhyme? How could you link the Title and Ending Phrase to give your poem a sense of order and completion?

2) Working in a group, modify your program so that it generates poetry instead of curses. Within your group, select your three favorite computer-generated poems.

3) Try making a program that generates haikus. A haiku is a short Japanese poem that consists of 3 lines. The first and last lines of a Haiku have 5 syllables and the middle line has 7 syllables. The lines rarely rhyme.

4) Make a Dadaist poem in the style of Tristan Tzara:

a. Take a newspaper.

b. Choose an article as long as you are planning to make your poem.

c. Make a list containing each of the words that make up this article.

d. Make a poem by randomly choosing each word. Remove the word from the list after it is used.

e. The poem will be like you.

*****Insert Poem here

```
when        clicked
go to x: 0 y: 0
point in direction 90▾
clear
pen down
move 100 steps
turn ↻ 90 degrees
move 100 steps
turn ↻ 90 degrees
move 100 steps
turn ↻ 90 degrees
move 100 steps
turn ↻ 90 degrees
turn ↺ 45 degrees
move 70 steps
turn ↻ 90 degrees
move 70 steps
```

Problem

Solutions

A1

2: First Program

1) There are many ways to draw a house. The code below shows one way to draw a house by first drawing the rectangle and then adding a triangle to the top of the image.

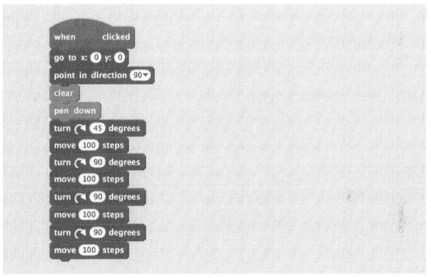

```
when       clicked
go to x: 0 y: 0
point in direction 90▾
clear
pen down
turn ↻ 45 degrees
move 100 steps
turn ↻ 90 degrees
move 100 steps
turn ↻ 90 degrees
move 100 steps
turn ↻ 90 degrees
move 100 steps
```

2) A diamond can be drawn in many ways. The code below shows a simple way to draw a diamond.

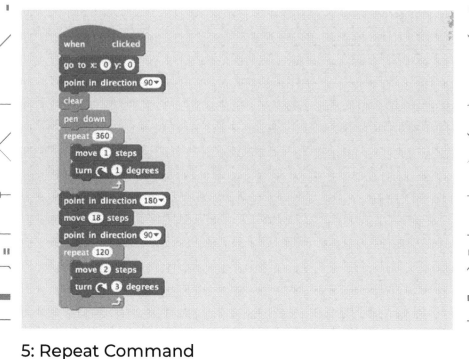

5: Repeat Command

1) There are many ways to draw different size circles.

The code below shows one way to draw two different size circles. The first repeat code draws the smaller inner circle and the second repeat code draws the bigger outer circle.

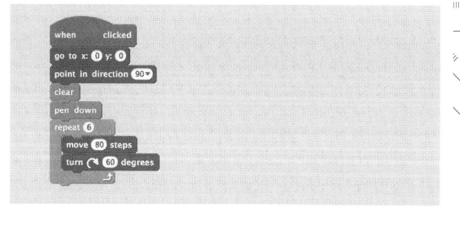

2) The easiest way to draw a hexagon is to draw 6 lines with an angle of 60 degrees between each line.

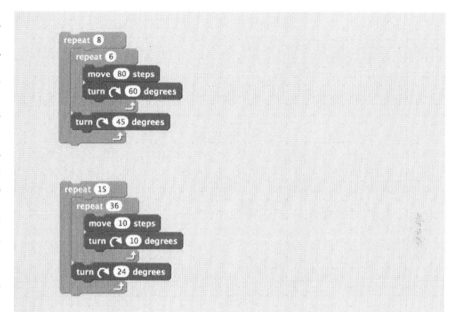

```
repeat 8
    repeat 6
        move 80 steps
        turn ↻ 60 degrees
    turn ↻ 45 degrees

repeat 15
    repeat 36
        move 10 steps
        turn ↻ 10 degrees
    turn ↻ 24 degrees
```

Nested Repeats

1) There are many ways to draw a shape consisting of hexagons. The code below describes one way to draw the shape.

2) The code below describes one way to draw a shape made out of many circles.

All About Variables 1) False. Since the computer thinks lower and upper-case letters are different, 'myFirstVariable and 'MYFIRSTVARIABLE do not mean the same thing to the computer.

2) The final value of w is: 12

3) The final value of w is: 16

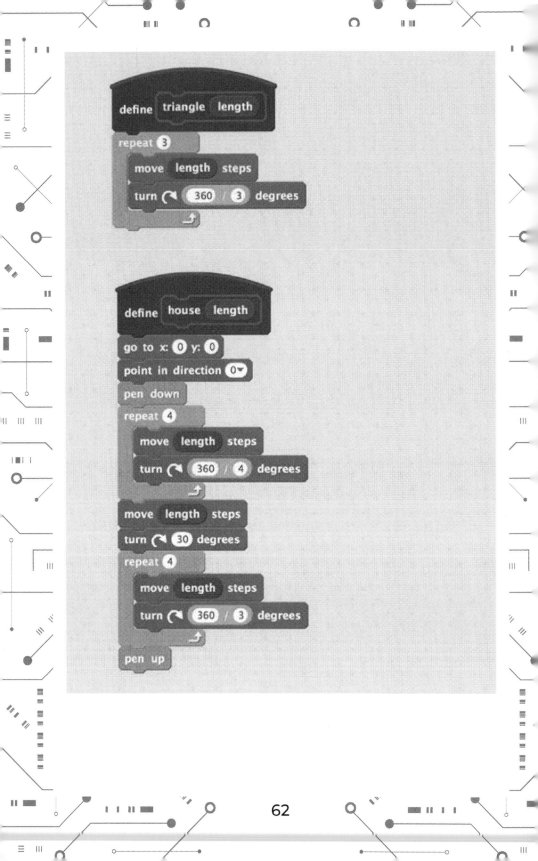

```
define triangle length

repeat 3
    move length steps
    turn ↻ 360 / 3 degrees
```

```
define house length

go to x: 0 y: 0
point in direction 0▾
pen down
repeat 4
    move length steps
    turn ↻ 360 / 4 degrees
move length steps
turn ↻ 30 degrees
repeat 4
    move length steps
    turn ↻ 360 / 3 degrees
pen up
```

CHAPTER - 4
LOOP THE HOOP

Have you been to a circus or a local festival where they have rides and things for everyone? Or you might have seen one on TV. The fancier merry-go-rounds have horse rides that also move up and down as you go around in circles. It was one of the things I loved the most when I was a kid. It was all fun and not scary at all! The ride goes round and round and round, endlessly and it has just the right speed.

In programming, we also have things that go round, round, and round! They are called loops. Yes, just loops, not the froot loops everyone loves! With loops we can do one or more tasks several times.

There are essentially two kinds of loops:

1. Loops that run for a specific number of times. We set the counter when creating the loop.

2. Loops that run until a specific condition is met. We define that condition when creating the loop.

We are going to work on two projects. Each project will focus on one type of the loop.

Loop #1

Have you ever taken a ride in a helicopter? Helicopters are so cool and scary at the same time. I loved helicopters. I have never been on a helicopter but as a kid, I used to be a helicopter enthusiast. I collected helicopter models and read books about them. I think I was inspired by the 80s TV show Airwolf. Okay, let me be clear. I am not that old and there's nothing wrong with watching very old TV shows, especially when they are as unique as Airwolf.

You know what's even cooler than helicopters? Spaceships! The first time I saw a spaceship was in a movie. I don't remember what the name of the movie was but it made a lasting impression on me. Well, not everyone can go on spaceships. Technology is still not that advanced! But, that doesn't mean we can't imagine hopping onto a spaceship and cruising along an alien planet's surface. You know what, let's do that!

Create a new project, name it "Third Project" and add a backdrop named "Space". Add a "Rocketship" sprite. Make sure it is selected in the "sprite and backdrop" section and change the direction of the sprite to 139:

Now, making sure the "Rocketship" sprite is still selected, start adding the following blocks (in the exact same order):

1. Add "when   clicked" block from the "Events" options in the Code tab.

2. Add "go to x:124 y:107" block from the "Motion" options in the Code tab. Change the x value to -176 and y value to 107.

3. Now, from "Control" options in the same Code tab, add the block that looks like this (change the 10 to 70):

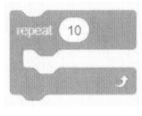

4. Inside the jaw of the above loop block, place a "change x by 10" block which is found in the "Motion" options in the Code tab. Change the 10 to 8.

5. From the "Sound" options in Code tab, drag the "start sound space ripple" and place it inside the loop block after the motion block.

The final stack will look like the image below.

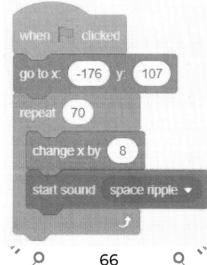

The stage may look like this before running the project:

Now, run your project by clicking on the green flag and see the spaceship speed through the night sky of this alien planet with very mysterious sci-fi sound effects!

Loop #2

The loop we used in the previous project will run 70 times because we set that value in the loop. What if we don't know the exact number when creating the loop? For example, if you run the above project, you will see that the spaceship actually flies off the screen. What if we want to run the loop until our sprite touches the edge of the stage?

Let's see how we can do that. Let me introduce my health-conscious friend, Avery, who needs our guidance while walking around the city streets. Let's create a fun little project to help Avery walk on city streets without wandering out too far.

Let's create a new project. If the previous project

is still open, make sure to save it before creating a new project. Name the new project "Fourth Project" and start making the following changes.

1. Choose the "Colorful City" backdrop.

2. Select the "Avery Walking" sprite. Change the size to 40. Change the x and y values to x: -220 and y: -123. The sprite setting should look like this.

Now, we have to add some blocks to this Avery.

1. Add "point in direction 90" block from the "Motion" options in the Code tab.

2. Add "go to x:124 y:107" block from the "Motion" options in the Code tab. Change the x value to -213 and y value to -123.

3. Now, from "Control" options in the same Code tab, add the block that looks like this:

4. In the hollow box of this loop block, put the block "touching MOUSE-POINTER" block. Change MOUSE-POINTER to EDGE.

5. Inside the same loop block, add a "change x by 10" block from "Motion" options under the Code block. Change 10 to 2.

The block stack should look like this.

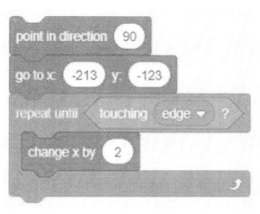

Now, we need to duplicate this whole block. Right click on this and select "Duplicate". It will create another block stack. Place it anywhere on the workspace with a left click. We need to change the settings on the second stack like below:

1. Change "point in direction 90" to -90

2. Change "go to x: -213 y: -123" to 216 and -123

3. Change "change x by 2" to -2

After the stacks are adjusted, put "when clicked" block from the "Events" options in the Code tab at the top of the entire stack. When you are done, the entire stack would look like this:

This whole stack will help Avery move from one end of the street to the other, turn around and then walk to the street end she started from. It is a very cool project. Save it with the name "Fourth Project" so you can help Avery whenever needed.

Loop within a Loop

The last thing we will learn is the secret of adding a loop block inside another loop block. Let's help Avery again because she wants to make at least 10 rounds on the street. Don't blame her, she wants to be healthy! We need to add one loop block to our Fourth Project and Avery will be able to walk up and down the city street.

We are going to use the loop#1 type and wrap most of the blocks inside them like shown in the image below. We are going to use 5 as the number of times the loop will execute.

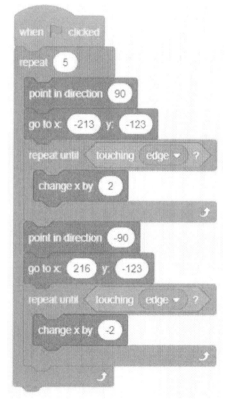

CHAPTER - 5

MOVE YOUR SPRITE!

Sprite Information
Below the Stage area, you will find the Sprite information box. Here you will find the Sprites you have added to your game already. This box also has information about each of them. Each Sprite has a name, and it is displayed in this information area. Scratchy's name is written as Sprite1. Boring right? You can change this name to something more fun if you want. You can also find information about the position of the Sprite and the direction it is facing.

Task: Making A Sprite Move

Let us start with an easy one: making a sprite move. To make Scratchy the cat move, follow these steps:

1. Go to the blocks palette and select the "motions" palette. Drag a "goto x: 0 y: 0" block and drop it in the script area.

2. Next, choose the "move ten steps" block and add

it to the bottom of the block.

3. Change the ten steps to 100 steps. Click the green button and see what happens. Nothing right? What seems to be the problem here? By using the motions block, Scratchy can now walk. But the poor cat doesn't know yet. So how do we tell Scratchy he can move now? That's very simple too.

4. Go to the "events" pallet. We want Scratchy to move, but we have first to tell Scratchy when to run. If we don't do this, Scratchy will not be able to move.

5. Click and drag the "when the green flag is clicked" blocked into the script area. Attach the motion blocks to the base of this new block. By doing this, you are telling Scratch that he can move when someone clicks on the green button.

6. Now click the green button again and see what happens. Congratulation. You just got scratchy to move. Now let's go over what you just did again.

Now let's talk about the motion blocks you used. The first block: "go to x: 0 y: 0," tells Scratch to move on the same line as it is. This follows a rule known as the coordinate system. I will explain what the coordinate system does soon. The last block tells the cat to take 100 steps. You can edit this to be any number of steps that you want, and Scratchy will bring that number of steps in the direction you have selected with the first block.

Understanding Position and Direction In Scratch.

Before we make the cat turn around, let's learn about positioning and direction in Scratch. First, go to the box beneath the stage and choose a new backdrop. On the list of backdrops, you will find a sprite named XY-grid. Select this Sprite. You should notice the background of your stage area transform into a box with lines and numbers. This will help you understand the coordinate system that Scratch uses to position objects. What is the number at the center of the two lines crossing each other? (x:0 and y:0) right?

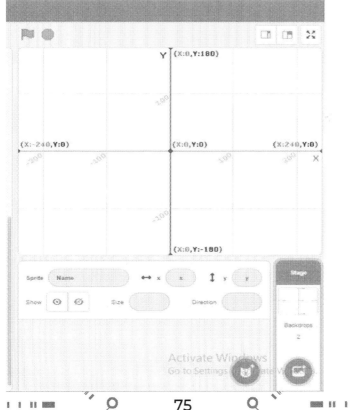

To understand what this means, you need to get familiar with the grid system. You've probably been thought that in school. But even if you have not been taught, it is straightforward to understand. Just follow along with In a grid system. Everything is positioned on two axes. The Y-axis represents the line that goes from up to down. This marks the up and down (vertical position) of any object. The Y-axis is labeled form -180 (at the lowest part of the lines) to 0 at the middle to +190 at the top of the page.

The X-axis represents the line that goes from left to right. This indicates the position of an object on a horizontal line. It has a range from -240 on the left and +240 on the right.

Task: Let's Try Some Positioning Examples

Now for some cases: if we set the value of Scratchy's position as (x: 0 and y:180), what does that mean? It means we want Scratchy to be positioned at the top of the page vertically without leaving the center. Scratchy will move up vertically without going left or right. Let's look at other examples:

(x:-240 and y:180): try to guess what this means; this says scratchy should be positioned at the top of the page and the farthest left side of the page. The Sprite will end up on the top left corner of the page.

Here's another example: (x:90 and y:50)- this

command says Scratchy should move by 90 places to the right and move 50 spaces up.

Let us look at one final example: (x:-100 and y:-80) try guessing what this command says: This command simply tells Scratchy to move to the left by -100 spaces while going down by 80 areas.

Before we proceed, let's try to change something in the previous code we wrote and see how this will affect Scratchy, the cat. Go to the Script area and select the "go-to" block. Edit the figures on the box to (x:90 and y:90). Do not change anything else. Click on the green button now and see what happens. Notice that the cat did not move in the same direction as it did before. You can try out different combinations of X and Y and see how your Sprite responds.

Now that you can see how scratch positions objects, we can proceed to learn more about moving the Sprites in different directions with the motion blocks.

Turning And Waiting

Let's add some more blocks to your code to make the Sprite change direction. For a simple task, we are going to make the cat move around in a square. This should be easy and fun.

Step 1: Go back to the motions block palette and select the "turn counterclockwise 15 degrees" block. Drag and add this to the bottom of the blocks you had before. Change 15 to 90 degrees. At this stage, you can click the green button to see how Scratchy reacts or continue with the rest of the instructions.

Step 2: Add three more blocks like this.

Step 3: Click the green button and see what happens. The cat moved in a square, but you probably didn't notice before it was quite fast. Let fix that as I introduce you to another category of blocks.

Wait For Blocks

Select the "controls" palette on the block tab. Click and drag the "wait for 1-sec" block into the script area. Do the same thing for each of the turns. Doing this will add a wait of 1 sec before the cat follows the next command. This will show each step as the cat changes direction more clearly. You can change the wait time to make it even slower if you want to. That was cool, wasn't it? Let's try some new tricks with the things we have learned so far.

More motion blocks

What if we wanted to make Scratchy glide about instead of jumping the way he did before? How do you think we can do that? Let's go back to the motions palette and see if there's anything there that can make Scratchy glide around. Can you find anything that helps? Yes. The "glide" block can be used to make Scratchy glide smoothly across the screen from one position to another.

To do this, follow these instructions:

I Step 1: Remove all the blocks we used earlier, leaving only the "when the green flag is clicked" block.

I Step 2: Now drag in the "glide _ secs to x:0 y:0".

I Step 3: You can edit x and y position as you want it. You can also change the time from one second to any time of your choice. This will change how fast the Sprite will guide to the position you have chosen.

Once you are done editing, click the green flag to see what happens. You can play around with other action buttons and see what other cool stuff you can make scratchy do,

LOOPS: MAKING THE SPRITE REPEAT AN ACTION.

Before we proceed, let's quickly learn a neat new trick that will be very helpful as you learn to code more with Scratch. Like every other programming language, the more you make Scratch do, the longer your codes you need to write.

For instance, remember the code we wrote to make Scratchy the cat moves in a square while waiting for 1 second after each turn. It was a simple "move-turn-wait" code. But the code became quite long because this action was repeated four times for scratchy to move in a square.

Imagine if we wanted the character to move like

these 100 times, we would need to join 1200 blocks to make that happen. That's a lot of hard work, right? We don't want to waste our time on that kind of hard work. Luckily, there is a neat little trick that can make your codes shorter and still make the character do what we want over and over again. In coding, this is what is called a loop. To do this in Scratch, all you need is a repeat block.

Remember the blocks we combined with moving the cat in a square earlier. Now we need it again. Along with the when the green button is clicked block, you should have five blocks. To make Scratchy repeat this same move four times, drag a "repeat" block from the "controls" palette into the script area. Put all the "move-wait-turn" blocks into the repeat block and set how many times you want the action to be repeated. Since we want the cat to move in a square, we can set this value to 4 instead of 10. now, when you click on the green flag, the cat will run on its own and repeat the action for the set number of times.

Let take things a step further. Let's take a look at our code and see any repeated action that we can set into a loop like this one. For instance. Remember that in the first motion block we set the cat to move 100 steps. How about we make it move 10 steps at a time. How many times will the Sprite move now to complete 100 steps? Yeah. You are a smart kid. The cat will run 10 times instead of 100 times now. But we don't want to waste our time repeating ten move blocks. So what can we do? I know, we can summon the loop wizard again.

This time remove the moving block from the rest of the blocks. Change the number of steps to 10. Select a repeat block from the palette and drag it into the script area. Put the "move" block into the repeat block and set the number of times you want this action to be repeated. Join the other blocks as you had it before. Click the green flag to see what happens. You should see the Sprite move smoothly across the screen in a square.

More on Loops

Before we move on from loops. Let's learn another neat trick:

A wizard is in town and has cast a spell on Scratchy, the cat. Now Scratchy will keep on moving in a square forever. The wizard used Scratch to cast this spell, do you want to know how to do this too. It's very simple. You can make a character in your game do the same thing over and over again using a forever loop block. It is just like the repeat block, but it has no end. Let see this in action. Remove the repeat block from your script. Replace this repeat block with the forever block. Click on the green flag and watch scratchy go on forever.

CHAPTER - 6

CREATING A PLAN FOR YOUR PROJECT

Many people don't like this concept. The worst thing that you can do when starting a project is to just jump in and start working on it. Instead of doing that, you should think about your project beforehand.

The Importance Of Having A Plan

First, consider a story. You could just open up scratch and then build your story as you go. You could pull up character sprites, and just make up stuff for the characters to say. You could keep doing this until you had a large number of scenes worked out.

There might be a better way to come up with a story app for your scratch project. Suppose that instead of just working it out on the fly, you took some time to think about your story first. You could even use a pencil and paper. Start by drawing the main characters. Or you can just write down their names and what they look at.

Think hard about the characters in your story. Who

are they and where do they come from? What do they want?

Then build up an overall outline for the story. At this stage, you don't have to fill in all the details. Just outline the main points of the story. You could name each scene you would like to have, and then write out what is going to be said and how things are going to develop. You can also write down some ideas about how each scene is going to transition into the next scene.

Again, this does not mean that you can't change the story later on. You can even change it after you have built up all the scenes in scratch. It can be changed at any time. But by planning, we will find that we save a lot of time and energy, and our work usually turns out better than it would if we just rushed ahead with it on the computer.

The More Complex the App, The More Planning You Need

If you are going to design a complicated game, it can help to use the same procedure. If you are building a script that is going to be really complicated, then it is even more important to plan out how you are going to do it first. The worst thing that you could do is jump on the computer and just start trying to build a game or large application without having any idea about how it's going to work and progress.

Let's say that you wanted to make a maze game. A

good way to approach this is to draw out all of your mazes on paper before you even open up scratch. You might find that some mazes that look good on paper are too hard to get through when you actually put them up on the computer screen. But one thing for sure is that your building of the game is going to be accomplished in a much shorter time once you get on the computer in scratch than if you had not planned it out ahead of time.

Planning Is Best as A Middle Ground

You want to plan out your programs, but don't overdo it. You don't want to write down every last detail. Have you written any papers in school? The way to write a paper is to start by making an outline. You can think of that here. Think of your planning stages for coding as making an outline for your project. Then when you actually start working on it on the computer and building your scripts, you can fill in all the details and potentially make changes.

Use the Planning Stage To Hone Your Ideas

During the planning stage, talk to others that are using scratch, or to your friends. Discuss your ideas with them to see what they think and see if they have some ideas that can make your project even better. It is easier to work things out like this in the planning stage if you are working on a large project. If you dive in to building your project and have a large number of sprites and scripts, having to go into all that detail to make major changes to the scripts can be very time consuming and frustrating. If you are working on a really large project, the project can actually get so complex that it is nearly impossible to change.

Planning with Pseudo Code

When we are working with scratch, we create actual code in our scripts. It can be helpful to plan out your scripts ahead of time by writing what is called pseudocode on a piece of paper. All this means is that you write out the steps that are going to be used in your script. So, we can write something like this:

If a cat touches the green bar then

· Play meow sound

· Increase score by one point

So, in other words, we are basically thinking out and

writing down the steps that our program is going to take ahead of time. This is an informal process, and so you don't need to have all the steps laid out exactly.

Think of the time you will save by doing this, though. When you write all the steps out, then opening up scratch and actually building the scripts is going to be so much easier that you are going to be amazed.

Start with The End Goal in Mind

Start the planning process with two statements. First, write down the starting point of your project. Then, write down the endpoint or goal of the project. So, if someone were to use your application, what is the end result of them doing so? This exercise should be used each time that you decide to start a new project on scratch. Once you have the two endpoints clearly defined, then filling in the intermediate steps to get you from point A to point B is a lot easier.

Draw Scenes on Paper

Don't just write out pseudocode when planning out your project. You can actually draw out the scenes the way you want them to look. Are you a lousy artist? Don't worry about that if you are. The point of doing this is not to impress anyone with your artistic ability. You don't even have to show the drawings to anyone else if you don't want to. The point of doing the drawings is for you and to help you get organized and get your project done faster and more efficiently. People who don't plan things out this way can end up wasting a lot of time in front of the computer screen. Wouldn't you rather be efficient and get your work done fast? It will also help you reduce frustration because you can open up your project and start building it quickly, according to the plan that you have already laid out.

Scheduling Your Work

You can also create a calendar and schedule for your project. You can specify what you are going to do on each of the days on the calendar. This will help you work more efficiently, which means that you will get more done in less time.

Reasons to Code

There are many different reasons that we can put forward for kids to learn to code. The first is that there is a continued shortage of people who are able to fill STEM jobs. Millions of these jobs are going unfilled, and a shortage means higher wages for those that possess the needed skills.

Learning some coding skills early is something that children can do to help bolster their resume in these competitive times. Even getting into college, or at least the college that you want is something that can be made easier if the child can already demonstrate some practical skills.

Coding can also help children understand the technical world that is all around them. They can understand the internet, smart TVs, and smartphones they can't seem to put down. By understanding how things work, they can also begin to get inspired and think of their own ideas.

Coding Can Make You Smarter And Improve Your Self-Confidence

You have probably seen people that go to the gym and exercise a lot. People that lift weights gain a lot of muscle. Other people that run or ride bikes get stronger and healthier. It turns out that the brain works in the same way. Your brain is just like a muscle. If you sit around and don't exercise at all, your muscles will shrink from a lack of use, and the body becomes weak. Older people who never exercise get out of breath just walking around.

The same thing happens to your brain. If you don't use it, then it won't develop and become strong. But if you work your brain by challenging it, the brain becomes stronger, literally making you smarter. The more you work your brain, the smarter you are going to get.

You may notice that if you practice doing math problems, they get easier for you. Or the more you study for an exam, the easier it is to remember what you need to know. And you become more confident about the right answers.

Coding is one of the best ways to challenge your brain and help you become smarter. Although people who haven't gotten any experience doing computer coding find it scary, when you take it slow and learn it step-by-step, you find out how natural it really is. Computer coding is nothing more than doing what comes naturally to humans. Let me explain.

What made the difference? Our brains made the difference. In other words, we used our ability to think. People used their minds to think of better ways to do things. This led them to figure out that they could survive cold nights by using animal skins to make clothing. Then they devised strategies to hunt, allowing them to use thinking for hunting the animals they needed to eat rather than trying to track them down using sheer speed and strength. They also invented many tools, to help them hunt using spears and arrows, and to cut things so they could use what they found in the environment, including preparing food to eat. Long ago, someone figured out how to use fire as another way of staying warm at night, and also to keep dangerous animals away.

This has been going on throughout history. People have continued to find out new and better ways of doing things, and this helped create civilization. This process is still going on today.

It turns out that computers are a natural fit for the

human mind, even though at first people don't feel this way about them. Computers are really just an extension of the human mind, and coding is just step-by-step problem-solving. So, it's not any different than any of the activities people have always engaged in.

When you get to work building a computer program, you are exercising the muscles of your brain, engaging in problem-solving activities. The more you do it, the better you are going to get at problem-solving. Coding teaches you to think carefully and to consider everything that can impact the problem at hand. It will also teach you how to look at how things will change, as each step in a computer program is executed. Not everyone has the same abilities, so some people are going to be better computer programmers than others. But that isn't what's important. The thing to remember is that everyone is going to be smarter than they were before they tried coding if they devote some time to learning this valuable skill.

The more you learn, the better your programming and problem-solving skills become. You can start off building simple programs, and then each time you tackle a new problem. You can build a more complex program.

CHAPTER - 7
ADVANCED CONCEPTS

After completing more than 10 projects in this book, it is time to focus on a few concepts in theory. We are going to discuss some advanced things here kiddo, but you can do it! Believe me, even many adults find these concepts hard to grasp.

Scratch is one of a kind when it comes to programming techniques. In Scratch, you use blocks to solve problems and create new things, an approach called block-oriented programming. Do you know what the most popular programming languages are? According to Stackify, here's the top three from 2019:

1. Java

2. C

3. Python

Guess what? None of them use block-oriented

programming. There are other approaches to programming, and we are going to discuss them now.

Functional Programming

Functional programming revolves around, drum roll please, functions! Remember our "Fifth Project", where we helped Gandalf find his magic stuff? We duplicated the same set of blocks for all the four arrow keys. It was not very efficient, was it? Creating functions is a way to cut down the number of blocks (or number of script lines) and avoid repetition.

How do we do that? We identify the line of codes that we will be using more than once. We give it a function name so whenever we need to execute it, we just call that name. There's one other amazing thing about functions. You can give them input (multiple if you can) and they return an output. A real-life example is a washing machine. You put in clothes, liquid detergent, and sometimes coins. The machine also takes water from an intake and washes all the clothes. After a preset amount of time, the machine gives you the clothes washed, rinsed and sometimes dried. Keep in mind that a washing machine can wash different types of clothes.

It would not be wrong to say that functions are mini programs within the main program. Breaking a big program into smaller functions also improves readability. But sometimes it can make it harder to understand the flow of the program. The key is to identify if there's a need for a function.

Twist

Now, here's a twist. You can create a block in Scratch that behaves like a function. How do you do that? This is something you will have to learn after you become good at things we have covered in this book. For now, add this to your to-do list.

Object-Oriented Programming

This is another type of programming, where everything is considered an object. Variables, constants, and even functions are just objects, or part of an object. This concept is closest to real-life and most applications built to tackle real-life problems are built using this approach.

Now, let us take the example of Cooper, the dog. He has many characteristics: he's (super) cute, friendly, talkative, happy and lovable. When it comes to doing stuff (actions), he can wag his tail, jump, walk, eat, hug, kiss, and lick among many other things. In the world of programming, Cooper is an object. His characteristics are called attributes. His actions are called modules (a fancy word for functions). We can give the object instructions to get some output.

We can also use, change, and transfer the available attributes. I know there's a saying you can't teach an old dog new tricks, but Cooper is a young fellow and we can definitely teach him some new tricks. This is equivalent to adding new modules to an object.

Algorithms and Flowcharts

When you advance in programming, you will see that it is difficult to keep up with the details and flow when a code starts to grow big. To help programmers keep track of everything, there is an entire process used when writing complex programs. Programmers write what is called an algorithm before writing the actual code.

An algorithm is a list of instructions that is written before coding is started. It helps break down the problem into groups of actions. Algorithms are actually used to detail the solution of the problem in simple human language. It also helps programmers to remain on task because sometimes it's easy to lose focus. Algorithms can be written for any task. For example, write a step-by-step guide on how to get ready for school in the morning.

Although not as popular anymore, veteran programmers still work with a flowchart, mostly to show non-technical colleagues how the program/application will be created. This is a bit more technical than writing algorithms because the shapes used to represent each step must match the type of action happening in that step. But this makes much more sense to view a flowchart because it gives a clear understanding of the flow of a program. Flowcharts are also used by planning teams to lay out a plan. If you have used MS Excel, you might have seen the flowchart section when you opened the Insert Shapes menu.

Health is Happiness

Why are we talking about health? Because health does matter. Talk with an old person and they'll tell your health is the most precious thing in this world. Here's a secret for your kiddo: if you have health, you can do anything. Spending a lot of time in front of screens can lead to various health concerns, especially those related to the eyes. In today's world, kids are also not spending too much time outdoors. It may lead to weaker muscles and immune system.

I am going to tell you a few tips that you can follow to keep your health in top condition.

The 20-second Rule

The rule is simple: for every 20 minutes spent in front of a computer, cellphone or a tablet screen, you should look at an object that's 20 feet away for 20 seconds. Why is that a good idea? Because you use your eye muscles to focus on a certain object. When you focus on a nearby object, your eye muscles remain strained. If you keep looking for a long time, the muscles get tired. It is for this reason that your eyes feel weary after spending a couple of hours looking at a handheld device. When you look at an object that's far away, your eye muscles get time to relax. This will help you a lot because many adults spend around 15 hours of each day in front of a screen. It is possible you would be doing the same when you grow up even when you don't want to. This is because of work requirements. The 20-second rule will help you avoid strained and sore eyes.

Hydration is Key

How much fluid do you drink in a day? The best fluid you can drink is water, because it has no bad stuff such as sugar. Using a computer or handheld smart device is fun and many times distracting. You lose focus and sense of time. This can lead to reduced hunger and thirst which is very bad for your health. What we can do is whenever you take the break for the 20-second rule, drink some water. Now, everyone has different requirements depending upon their age. Ask an adult how much water you should drink in a day.

When you start drinking more water, you will need to pee more. This feels like a nuisance but is very crucial to clean your body. Do not hold up, you should go to the bathroom as soon as you feel the need to do so.

When I talk about hydration, it's not just about drinking fluids. Your eyes also require good hydration levels for proper function. Have you ever experienced redness or itching after spending a long time in front of a screen? The phenomenon is pretty unique. Do you know why you blink? Blinking is an automatic process where your body removes dust and other things from the eyes and rehydrates the eyes. Have you ever noticed that sometimes when you are focusing on a screen, you forget to blink and only realize it after a few minutes? When you don't blink, the dust doesn't get cleaned up and rehydration also doesn't happen. In short, don't forget to blink.

Running and Exercise

You might already be active enough, but make sure you allocate enough time for physical activities. When you sit for a long time, the muscles in your legs become weaker. The joints also lose their strength. These will take a long time to happen and that's why these are very dangerous. You will slowly slip into a routine and when you start to notice the bad things, the internal damage might already be beyond repair. Stretching exercises are a great way of relaxing muscles. I know it sounds wrong, but stretching does relax the muscles. A doctor can give a good answer on how it works.

Going out also changes your perspective. It is a great way to relax your mind so it can get out of pressure situations. Sometimes when you think too hard for too long, the creative process gets stuck. In such situations, it is good to take a break, go outside to play or run.

Now, I understand that as a kid it is very difficult to go outside because you need permission and company. That's not a bad thing kiddo, trust me. Talk with your parents and let them know you need some of their time so they can go out with you. It is not like going out for a vacation. It won't require a lot of preparation. 20 to 30 minutes a day is good enough. It will give everyone some more time together and it will also benefit your parents' health.

Perfect Posture

There is a good way and a bad way to do every job in this world. Many people do things the wrong way because it's just easier. Using computers and handheld devices with the wrong posture is also another very easy pitfall to fall into. There are many parts of your body that cannot handle stress for a long period of time. These parts include your neck, your wrists, your spine, and ankles.

When you sit in front of a computer, make sure of following things:

1. Your feet are grounded firmly on the floor

2. Your thighs should be parallel to the floor

3. Your calves should be perpendicular to the floor

4. Your back should be relaxed and have a natural arc. The chair should provide support to your

back but must not push into it

5. The computer table should be on the same height as your arms

6. The computer screen should be on the same height as your eyes

7. The mouse should be light-weight

8. Keyboard should be soft-touch so you don't need to press them hard

I know these are a lot of rules. But they are very important. It will take time to follow all of them without effort. It also means you have to use the right kind of furniture. Again, that's not something you will be able to do yourself. Understandably, this is again something you should discuss with your parents. Chances are they already know about these but are not following them. Tell them the importance and the problems that can happen if you don't follow them for a long time.

CHAPTER - 8

DAY AND NIGHT GAME

Algorithms

You will soon learn how to create your own computer games. But first let's talk about Algorithms.

Have you ever given someone directions? Or explained how to make a sandwich? If so, then you're already familiar with algorithms.

Let's say you want to teach someone how to make a Club Sandwich.

The steps are usually as follow:

1. Take two slices of bread

2. Place a slice of ham over one slice of bread

3. Place a slice of cheese over the ham

4. place a second slice of bread on top of the cheese.

That's it!

We have a sequence of steps. Let's call the sequence: A step by step procedure, or script

The ordered sequence of steps is called an algorithm. Algorithms describe the procedure for solving a given problem.

Here is the algorithm you created in your very first game.

Movement and Talk Algorithm

- When Flag clicked
- Move 100 steps
- Say Greetings for 2 seconds
- Say How are you for 2 seconds

Reset Position Algorithm

- When spacebar key is pressed
- Move to position 0, 0 (middle)

Conditionals

To game the Day and Night game, you will make use of conditionals

What Are Conditionals

A conditional, simply put, is a condition for something to happen.

Let's take an example. If you have enough money

then you can buy some cakes. If you don't have enough money, then you can't.

With conditionals, you can tell computers to perform an action. If user click the spacebar key, then position the cat in the middle.

Another example, If it is night, then tell me it's Dark Outside,

Conditionals in Scratch

Scratch provides specific blocks to add conditionals to your game. You will use some simple one to build the Day and Night game, the If < > then block:

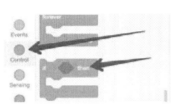

We will use this block for this next game, first let's create a new project.

Create A New Project

Click on File the top left and New:

This will create a new project, give it a name, let's call it "Day and Night".

Sprites

Creating a new game will again place the Cat in the middle of the Stage.

We want to use a different character for this game,

Let's remove the Cat.

Removing A Sprite

To remove a sprite, in this case the Cat, click on the small cross icon above the Cat sprite in the Sprite Area:

The cat disappeared from the Stage, we will now add a different Sprite.

Adding A Sprite

To add a new sprite, in the Sprite area, mouse over the + icon, and click the search button:

A screen will show with plenty of Sprites in the gallery, for this game need a Bat , find it and click on it:

You now have a Bat on the stage.

Backdrops

The backdrop is the background of your stage, it's rather boring to have a plain background, so let's add some a Colorful City background.

Adding A Backdrop

To add a backdrop, find the + icon on the right of the Stage panel, below the stage panel, and click the Search button: .

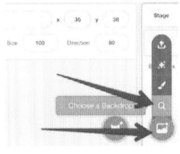

A screen will show with plenty of Backdrop in the gallery, this game needs a night and a day backdrop.

Search for a night image, find the Night City backdrops, add the it, then search again and find/ add Colorful City:

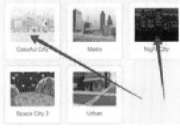

The stage will show the last drop you added. So, it should look like this:

Note: The backdrops can be found on the left side, just beside the Blocks panel, there is a Backdrop tab.

Click on it and see that there is a list of backdrops, one for the night city and one for the day city.

You can click on the backdrop you want by default, we want the Colorful City by default.

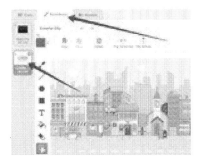

Game Logic

You now have all your arts put in the stage

A bat

A day backdrops

A night backdrop (not visible for now, but it's there)

This section is about making your backdrop change on a keyboard key press, and have the Bat tell you whether it is Bright or Dark outside.

First, let's go back to the Code tab.

You will now Switch the backdrop on Event.

Switch Backdrop on Event

To switch the backdrop, we will use Event block called when space key pressed, to make the backdrop switch to the other image.

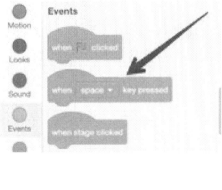

Drag it to the Scripting Area, then find and drag and plug, right below it, the next backdrop Looks Block:

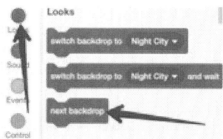

You should get a script like this in your Script Area:

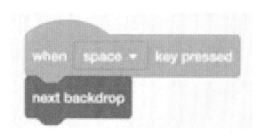

Test your stage, by pressing the spacebar key on your keyboard multiple times to make sure the backdrop changes from Day to Night and Night to Day.

A Note on Multiple Scripts

Observe that each script is associated with an element. When you created the script for the backdrop change, you selected the backdrop element, so the script is visibly only when the backdrop element is selected.

Click on the Bat in Sprite area, and you will see that the script you've created disappears,

Don't panic, it is still there, just click again on the backdrop in the backdrop area (on the left below the stage) and you will see your script appear again in the Script Area.

Make the Bat Talk

Click on the Bat sprite, in the Sprite Area.

Then find and drag the Event block called when this sprite clicked into the Script Area:

Then, find the say Hello! for 2 seconds block and plug it below the when this sprite is clicked block in the Script Area, you should get this:

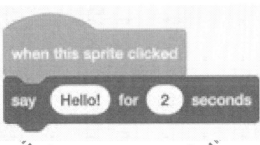

Then test, to see that when you click on the Bat, in the stage, the bat says Hello! for 2 seconds

MAKE THE BAT TALK CONDITIONALLY

We now need to make the Bat say "Hello, It's Bright outside" or

"Hello, It's Dark outside" depending on the backdrop that is shown in the stage.

To do that, find the Control block if < > then block:

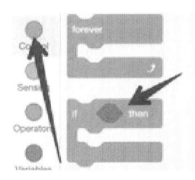

Then drag and plug it right blow the when this sprite is clicked block in the Script Area:

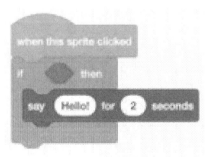

You might have to drag the Hello block away, to plug the If/then block, then plug the Hello block inside the If/then block, like shown above.

Now find the Operator equal block, in the Operator blocks:

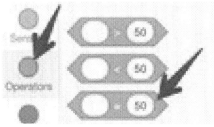

Then drag and plug inside the < > space inside the if/then block, like so:

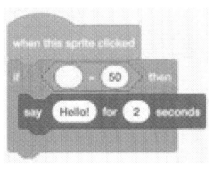

Then find the Look backdrop number block:

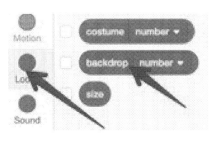

And drag/plug it on the left of the equal operator, like so:

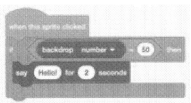

Finally:

Change the drop-down selected Number, to Name, on the left of the equal operator

Type   Colorful City instead of 50 on the right of the equal operator.

Replace Hello with Hello, It's Bright outside

You should obtain this script:

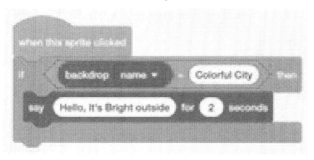

Now test, by clicking on the Bat with the night backdrop, and again with the day backdrop (remember it's the spacebar key on the keyboard to switch Backdrops).

The bat talks conditionally now, but it only talks when it's bright outside! Let's fix this.

Duplicate Script Blocks

The bat only has one condition: If it is the day backdrop, then   say Hello, It's bright outside.

We need to add another condition, which checks If the backdrop name represents the night backdrop, then the bat to say Hello, It's Dark outside.

To do so, let's duplicate the Bat script, and simply

change the name in the condition, and the message.

To duplicate, right click on the when this sprite clicked block, and click Duplicate:

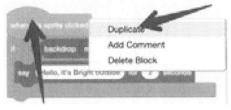

Drag the duplicated script below, like this:

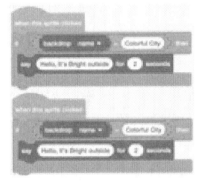

Now replace, in the duplicated script:

Colorful City to Night City

Hello, It's Bright outside to   Hello, It's Dark outside.

You should get this script:

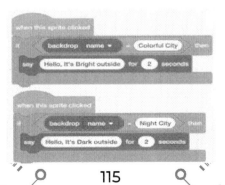

Event

Event blocks control events and the triggering of scripts. There are 8 Event blocks.

Input Events

When Green Flag Clicked — When the flag is clicked, the script activates.

When ( ) Key Pressed — When the specified key is pressed, the script activates.

When This Sprite Clicked — When the sprite is clicked, the script activates.

Situational Events

When backdrop switches to ( ) — When the backdrop switches to the one chosen, the script activates.

When ( ) is greater than ( ) — When the first value is greater than the second value, the script activates.

Control

Control blocks control scripts. There are 11 Control blocks.

Sprite Controls

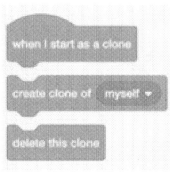

When I Start as a Clone (sprites only) — This block is triggered whenever a clone is created, and will only be run by that clone.

Create Clone of ( ) — Creates the specified clone.

Delete This Clone (sprites only) — Deletes a clone.

Loop Controls

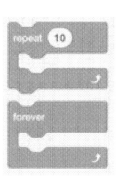

Repeat ( ) — A loop that repeats the specified amount of times.

Forever — A loop that will never end.

repeat until

Repeat Until ( ) — A loop that will stop once the condition is true.

Wait Controls

wait 1 seconds

Wait ( ) Secs — Pauses the script for the amount of time.

wait until

Wait Until ( ) — Pauses the script until the condition is true.

7.5.4. Conditional Controls

if then

if then
else

If ( ) Then — Checks the condition so that if the condition is true, the blocks inside it will activate.

If ( ) Then, Else — Checks the condition so that if the condition is true, the blocks inside the first C will activate and if the condition is false, the blocks inside the second C will activate.

Stop Script Control

Stop ( ) — Stops the scripts chosen through the drop-down menu. Can also be a stack block when "other scripts in this sprite" is chosen.

Sensing

Sensing blocks detect things. There are 20 different Sensing blocks.

Sprite Sensing Blocks

Touching ( ) ? — The condition for checking if the sprite is touching the mouse-pointer or another sprite.

Touching Color ( ) ? — The condition for checking if the sprite is touching a specific color.

Color ( ) is Touching ( ) ? — The condition for

checking if a color on the sprite is touching a specific color.

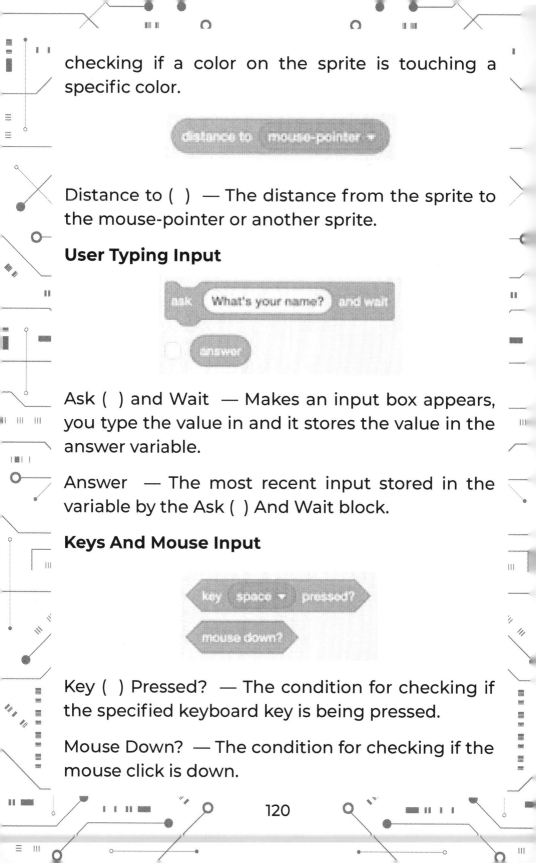

Distance to ( ) — The distance from the sprite to the mouse-pointer or another sprite.

User Typing Input

Ask ( ) and Wait — Makes an input box appears, you type the value in and it stores the value in the answer variable.

Answer — The most recent input stored in the variable by the Ask ( ) And Wait block.

Keys And Mouse Input

Key ( ) Pressed? — The condition for checking if the specified keyboard key is being pressed.

Mouse Down? — The condition for checking if the mouse click is down.

Mouse X — The mouse-pointer's X position.

Mouse Y — The mouse-pointer's Y position.

Draggable Sprite

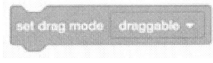

It can be used to drag a sprite in a project without needing a script for dragging.

Microphone And Time

Loudness — How loud the microphone noise is.

Timer — How much time has passed since the Scratch program was opened or the timer reset.

Reset Timer — Resets the timer.

Current ( ) — The specified time unit selected, can be from year unit to seconds. If ticked, it will display the value on stage.

Days since 2000 — The number of days since 2000.

Other Sensing Blocks

backdrop # ▾   of   Stage ▾

( ) of ( ) — The X position, Y position, direction, costume, size or volume of the Stage or a specific Sprite.

username

Username — The username of a user.

CHAPTER - 9

PRACTICING WITH SCRATCH

Although the logic behind programming is important, what is the use of logic if it is not put into practice?

In this section, you will find basic projects that you can complete within an hour or two. Be sure to take the time to understand the challenges and try to do them on your own before coming back and reading the solutions from the book. Remember that in programming: the process is more important than the outcome.

There is no one true way to achieve an outcome in programming. Yes, there may be more efficient and optimal ways, but in truth, it all boils down to whether, at the end of the day, you've achieved your goal or not. Similar to mathematics, where there are hundreds of ways to achieve the equivalent of two, accomplishing a certain goal in the world of programming can be achieved through various means.

Fall in love with the process, and do not be too fixated into the outcome.

Listed below are some of the projects taken from the internet that you could start working on right now; it will only take around 1-2 hours to complete each project.

Tron

If you're familiar with the game of Tron, then you know the simple mechanics of the game. In this game, you simply have to make sure that your character avoids the trail emitted by the other light cycles as well as your own by outmaneuvering the opposing players.

Here a few of the variables that you would have to take into account when making the game:

1. Movement

The movement for the game is simple and basic. You simply use your arrow keys to move your character around the map. However, it should be that the two characters are moving at the same time; neither one slows down or goes ahead of the other. If the player doesn't click an arrow key, then the sprite should just continue on the path that it was already on.

2. Hitting the trails or other sprites

Once your character hits a trail or the other sprite, then the game ends, and you lose. This also holds true in the case that a sprite hits the edge of the map. All of these are programmable using the blocks in Scratch.

3. Character

Your character should be set to be an individual on a bike. If the game ends, then either your character or the opponent becomes an "explosion" costume. So, in simpler terms, you just have to program the two sprites, their trails, and their respective icons in case the sprites touch the trails, the other bike, or the edges of the window.

Space Invaders

Space Invaders is another simple program that many beginner programs complete.

In this program, you simply shoot the oncoming aliens while you avoid their lasers. You will have three lives, and each time you get struck by an alien laser, then you lose a life.

In contrast to the original Space Invaders games, the alien ships do not approach you. Instead, they simply sweep from right to left, and it your job to destroy them.

This program will require you to set up the following variables:

1. Characters

There are two essential characters here, namely:

the player and the opponents. Now, both sides are represented by differing ships

2. Movements

The movements of the ships are simple, just shift left to right.

3. Lasers

Like the players, the lasers are representative of the opposing sides. Now, these lasers can be of any color, but I suggest picking totally opposing ones as this creates a better graphical user interface and a better gaming experience for the user.

4. Lives

A player is given three lives in this game. A counter should be visible, and each time a player gets struck by a laser, then the counter goes down by one.

Moon Landing

This program is most certainly more difficult than preceding projects.

In this program, we have to simulate landing a moon lander on the surface of the moon. If you land on anywhere but the landing pad, then your moon lander gets destroyed.

To make it easier, here are the things that you will need to have in your program:

1. Movement

Obviously, the movement will be an essential component of the whole project. In this game, you will have to be able to move your spacecraft left and right as well as up and down, taking into account that there is no air resistance in space. Once your character starts moving in one direction, then it should keep gliding in that direction.

2. Crashing

This is one of the simpler things that you will be programming. You will essentially need two costumes: the lunar lander sprite and the explosion costume. Since all of the rocks will be grey, then you simply have to create the program so that when the lunar lander sprite touches something grey, then it switches to the explosion costume before stopping the program, essentially meaning you lost.

3. Gravity

Like all planets, the moon has gravity, and this gravity pulls things towards the ground. Try to incorporate that into your code.

4. Landing

The goal of this program is such that when the lander touches the landing pad, the game ends. However, you could make it so that if the lander lands too fast on the landing pads, the ship falls apart.

Solutions

Now, You will find the solutions, but please remember that these aren't the only correct solutions. If you have come up with your own solutions (as many of you should have), then I congratulate you on your grit and determination! However, regardless of whether or not you had completed the projects by yourself, I still urge you to read the solutions here, for you might find better and more efficient solutions than the ones you made.

Tron

Here's a possible solution to the game:

1. Player Starting Position and Trails

These blocks of code set the starting position of the characters. The sprites labeled 'bike' are set to the position of (-175,0) while facing the 90-degree direction. From here, the following lines of code make it so that when the character is moved, then it would leave a pen trail of the specified color.

2. Crash Checker

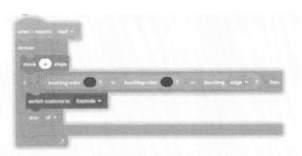

This is, as the name suggests, checks whether or not the sprite has "crashed." The blocks of code do so by checking the pen trail that the characters have left behind. If the character ends up touching his own pen trail or his opponent's, the sprite turns into the "explosion" character. If the character touches the other sprite, then they both transform into the "explosion" characters.

3. Player Movement

These lines of code control the movement of the characters. They control the direction that the character is moving. Because of the "pen up" and "pen down" blocks, the characters will continuously move unless told otherwise. As such, these blocks are meant more to direct the sprites rather than actually move them.

Space Invaders

1. Player

This is the main body of the program that basically describes the functionality of the player. Here, you will find that once you start the program, then you will be given two variables: Health and Points. The code will then continue to set the position of the sprite, choose a sprite, and show the variables.

The second half of the blocks of code is essentially the win-checker. Once either the player has obtained 5 points, or the player has lost all his lives, the game ends. Until then, the player will continue to move around by either pressing the right arrow key or the left.

2. Your Laser

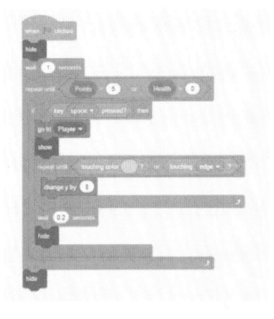

These lines of code explain how your laser works. Basically, if you press the spacebar, it will release a sprite in the form of the laser. If this sprite makes contact with the edge, it simply vanishes. If the laser makes contact with a yellow color, which is the color of the aliens, then it destroys them. Although it's not explicitly stated in this block of code, it will be stated in a different block.

3. Opponent

This is the block of code wherein you will find the functionality of the opponent aliens. It sets the starting position of the alien and creates its functionality, wherein the sprite would continue drifting left to right in a single direction until it hits the edges of the game. If the sprite gets struck by one of your lasers, then your point tally goes up, the sprite is replaced by an explosion sprite before vanishing.

4. Bad Laser

This is the portion of the program that controls the functionality of the "bad" lasers or, more appropriately, the lasers shot by the alien sprites. Essentially, the aliens shoot lasers at random intervals, and if they hit the player, the player loses a life. Otherwise, the laser simply disappears.

Moon Landing

1. Movement

This block of code simply moves the character around using the left, right, up, and down arrow keys. The logic behind this code is very similar to the logic behind the blocks for movement for Tron and Space Invaders. After all, movement is movement, and in most games, movement mainly pertains to the change in position of the sprite in relation to the background of the program.

2. Crash

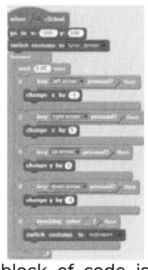

This additional block of code is responsible for checking whether or not the lander has crashed. It simply says that if the sprite touches the color gray, then it should switch to an "explosion" costume.

3. Movement

The change in these blocks of code simply shows that instead of changing the position of the sprite in relation to the background, we instead change the speed to simulate the presence of gravity in the program.

4. Up and Down

Similar to the change that you had input, you replace the code that is used for up and down movement so that instead of simply changing the position of the sprite in the program, we also try to simulate the presence of gravity in our program.

5. Landing

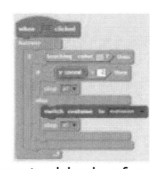

Finally, this separate block of code is used as a landing checker. It simply states that if the moon lander sprite touches a yellow color (the landing pad) but is moving slower than a speed of -2, then your sprite implodes on impact.

Looking at the solutions to the projects above, you'll find that the projects increase in difficulty. As you continue on your programming, you'll find that the projects that you create will require you to add more and more variables to your projects. The sheer complexity of the projects that you will soon be creating might seem daunting at first, but perseverance and determination will get you anywhere. Note, however, that these solutions above aren't the only solutions out there. It's best to try and come up with your own solutions! The library of programming solutions and concepts is so wide, and the variety of solutions that you can come up with are so plentiful.

Now this portion of the book has given you some increasingly difficult challenges. You do not need to accomplish the projects, but in doing so, you would have shown general mastery in the use of Scratch.

CHAPTER - 10

PROJECT-CONNECT FOUR

Connect Four is a 2-player game which consists of two sets of colored coins and a standing grid of rows and columns. Each player takes one set of coins and then by turn drops coins down any of the vertical columns (we will call them "tubes"). See the picture below.

The goal of the game is to get 4 coins of the same color to arrange themselves along a row, column, or diagonal. The first player to do this wins the game.

Do you want to check out a working Scratch version of this program? Click on the image below (or the URL just below it). I encourage you to explore the program and its various features. But, don't look at the Scratch scripts yet; we want to design this program ourselves!

How to Run The Program?

1. Click the "Green flag" to start the game.

2. Two users (blue and orange) will play the game by clicking alternately. The variable "Turn" shows whose turn it is.

3. Click the base of the tube in which you want to drop your coin.

4. Play until one of the players wins.

Scratch and CS Concepts Used

When we design this program, we will make use of the following Scratch and CS concepts. I assume that you are already familiar with these concepts.

Main concepts:

- Algorithms
- Arithmetic operators (+, -, *, /)
- Arithmetic expressions
- Backdrops - multiple
- Conditionals (IF)
- Events
- Geometry - parallel lines
- Logic operators (and, or, not)
- Looping - simple (repeat, forever)
- Looping - conditional (repeat until)
- Motion - absolute
- Motion - smooth using repeat
- Pen commands
- Relational operators (=, <, >)
- Sensing touch
- Sequence

- Sounds - playing sounds
- STAMP - creating images
- Synchronization using broadcasting
- User events (mouse)
- Variables - numbers
- Variables - strings
- Variables - properties (built-in)
- XY Geometry

Feature Idea # 1: Coins and the grid

Draw the coin sprites and the grid of vertical tubes.

Step 1: Draw the coin sprites.

Design:

To play the game we need lots of orange and lots of blue coins. But, how many sprites do we need?

Let us consider what happens to each coin. When a coin is dropped into a tube it just sits there until the game is over. So, we don't really need an actual coin sprite in the tube; an image would suffice. Does that give you some idea?

Yes, we can use the STAMP command to create an image of a coin when it is dropped in a tube. So, that means we just need two sprites: one for the orange coin and one for the blue coin. We will just draw the sprites.

Draw circle sprites with thick border. Fill them with gradient of the same color.

Resize them such that they fit the width of the tube.

Step 2: Draw the grid (series of tubes).

Design:

It is really up to us to decide how many tubes we should have. In my program, I have drawn 8 tubes. You can do the same or use a different number.

The grid, as you can see, has two parts:

1. A series of vertical lines which define the tubes

2. A solid base for each tube

The solid base of each tube will have to be a separate sprite, because, the players will select a tube by clicking its base. We can just draw one base and create duplicate sprites.

The vertical lines can be drawn as a sprite (or part of the background), but it is quite tedious to draw equidistant (equally spaced) parallel lines in the paint editor.

Instead, we will draw them in the program itself using the Pen commands and some simple geometry. First, we will draw the 8 bottom sprites and line them up in a straight line (see solution below).

The algorithm to draw the lines for the tubes is quite simple. Let's say "w" is the width and "h" is the height of each tube. Let's say point (x, y) is on the left edge of the first base.

Algorithm to draw the tubes:

```
Go to x, y
Repeat 9
    Pen down
    Change y by h
    Pen up
    Change y by -h
    Change x by w
End-repeat
```

Save as Program Version 1

Before continuing to the next set of ideas, we will save our project. This way, we have a backup of our project that we can go back to if required for any reason.

Compare your program with my program at the link below.

Connect4-1: includes idea 1 explained above.

How to run the program:

1. This program version doesn't do anything.

Next Set of Features/ideas:

Next, we will write scripts for dropping coins in the tubes. This involves the following features:

- choosing a tube

- choosing the right coin to drop

- positioning a coin on top of the selected tube

- dropping a coin down the selected tube

For this version, make a copy of your project (using "Save as") under a different name. For example, I am calling my copy as Connect4-2.

Let us get cracking with these ideas and features one by one.

Feature Idea # 2: Choosing tube and coin

Implement a way for the players to choose a tube, and have a way for the players to take turns.

Design:

Selecting a tube is straightforward. Since each tube has a separate base sprite, the players can simply click on the base to choose a tube.

To ensure players play by turn, we can have a variable called "Turn" which will indicate whose turn it is. If it says "orange" an orange coin will be dropped and if it says "Blue" a blue coin will be dropped.

Feature Idea # 3: Drop the coin

Write scripts to position the selected coin on top of the selected tube and drop it into the selected tube.

Step 1: Position the coin on top of the selected tube.

Design:

The variable "Turn" tells us which coin is to be dropped. The player will click on the base of the selected tube. In order to position a coin on top of this tube we need to know the X and Y co-ordinates of the point. We can pick some arbitrary value of Y which is somewhere above all tubes. How about X?

Well, we can use the X of the base sprite, right? Each base, when clicked, can save its X position in a variable.

Step 2: Drop the coin into the selected tube.

Design:

Making the coin drop into the tube is straightforward. We can make it move downward until it touches the base or another coin.

We don't need to leave the coin in the tube; we can leave its image. The STAMP command will come handy for that purpose.

Save as Program Version 2

Before continuing to the next set of ideas, we will save our project. This way, we have a backup of our project that we can go back to if required for any reason.

Compare your program with my program at the link below.

Connect4-2: includes ideas 2 and 3 explained above.

How to run the program:

1. Click the "Green flag" to start the game.

2. Two users (blue and orange) will play the game by clicking alternately. The variable "Turn" shows whose turn it is.

3. Click the base of the tube in which you want to drop your coin.

Final Set of Features/ideas:

We really have all the important features of the game working now. We will just add a few more features to make the program more tidy, robust, and user-friendly. Here are the things we will consider in this version:

- When a tube becomes full, don't allow coins to drop in it.

- Add a welcome screen.

- Add a help screen and sounds.

- Add code that will automatically place the pipe bases in a neat row.

For this final version, make a copy of your project (using "Save as") under a different name. For example, I am calling my copy as Connect4-final.

Let us get cracking with these ideas and features one by one.

Feature Idea # 4: Tube full condition

When a tube becomes full, don't allow coins to drop in it.

Design:

There are different ways to implement this feature. For example, you could keep a count of the number of coins inside each tube in a list variable, and check that count every time a coin is dropped.

I am going to use a much simpler idea which is as follows: Just start dropping the coin. After it reaches the lowest point, check its Y position and if it is more than a certain value (a point where the tube would look full), cancel the subsequent steps (i.e. creating its image etc.).

Do you like the idea?

If you do, modify your scripts to implement this idea.

Feature Idea # 5: Welcome and Help Screens

Add a welcome screen, a help screen and suitable sounds.

Design:

This should be a straightforward task. We will arrange the code such that the welcome screen appears when Green Flag is clicked and everything else is hidden at that time. After a short time (say 4 seconds) the game screen will appear.

The help screen will be optional – available when some key is pressed. It should go away when the mouse pointer is clicked anywhere.

What about sounds? Well, I have added one sound clip which plays every time a coin is dropped.

Feature Idea # 6: Placement of bases

Use a script to automatically place the bases in a neat row.

Design:

This is a matter of using the X-Y geometry and the "Go to x, y" command. Since all bases are at the same height, the Y position of all will be the same. Now, if you know the width of each base and the x position of the first base, can you calculate the x positions of the subsequent bases?

Here is the algorithm for these calculations:

```
Let x be the position of the first base.
Let w be the width of each base.
X position of the 2nd base = x + 1*w
X position of the 3rd base = x + 2*w
X position of the 4th base = x + 3*w
```

Do you get the idea? Now, since the sprites only move by themselves, each base will need to place itself when the Green Flag is clicked.

Save as the Final Program Version

Congratulations! You have completed the program with all the features we had planned. Save your program as "Connect4-final.sb2".

Compare your program with my program at the link below.

Connect4-final: includes ideas 4, 5, and 6 explained above.

How to run the program:

1. Click the "Green flag" to start the game.

2. Two users (blue and orange) will play the game by clicking alternately. The variable "Turn" shows whose turn it is.

3. Click the base of the tube in which you want to drop your coin.

Additional challenge

If you are interested, work on this additional challenge.

For idea #4 above, implement this alternate technique: Keep a count of the number of coins in each tube, and check that count every time. When the count reaches the upper limit, disallow adding any more coins. You could use a list variable for these counts.

Solutions to Feature Ideas

Feature idea # 1:

Step 1:

See the sprites below:

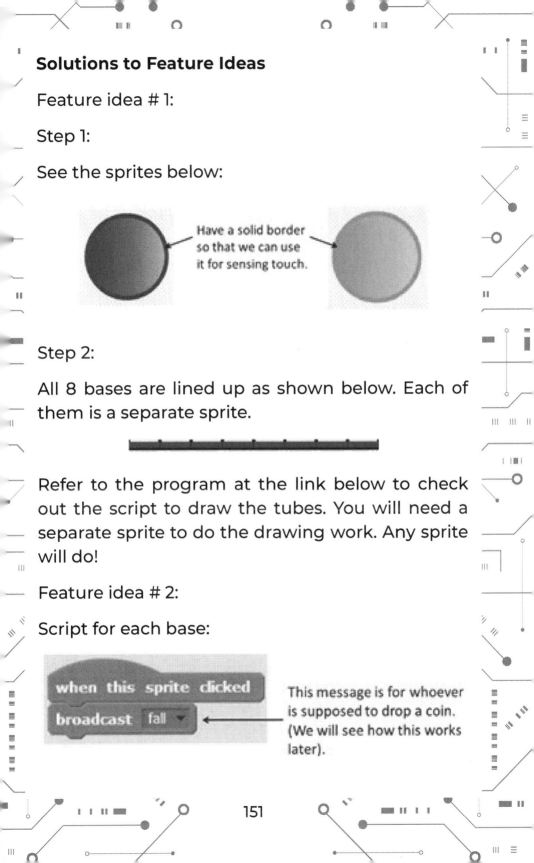

Have a solid border so that we can use it for sensing touch.

Step 2:

All 8 bases are lined up as shown below. Each of them is a separate sprite.

Refer to the program at the link below to check out the script to draw the tubes. You will need a separate sprite to do the drawing work. Any sprite will do!

Feature idea # 2:

Script for each base:

```
when this sprite clicked
broadcast fall
```

This message is for whoever is supposed to drop a coin. (We will see how this works later).

Feature idea # 3:

Step 1:

Modified script for each base:

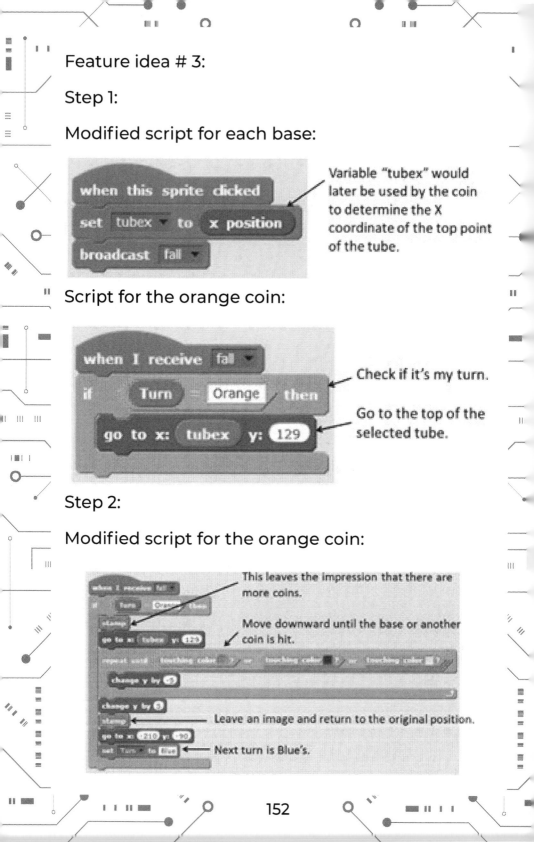

```
when this sprite clicked
set tubex to x position
broadcast fall
```

Variable "tubex" would later be used by the coin to determine the X coordinate of the top point of the tube.

Script for the orange coin:

```
when I receive fall
if   Turn = Orange   then
    go to x: tubex y: 129
```

Check if it's my turn.

Go to the top of the selected tube.

Step 2:

Modified script for the orange coin:

```
when I receive fall
if   Turn   Orange   then
    stamp
    go to x: tubex y: 129
    repeat until   touching color ?  or  touching color ?  or  touching color ?
        change y by -5
    change y by 5
    stamp
    go to x: -210 y: -90
    set Turn to Blue
```

This leaves the impression that there are more coins.

Move downward until the base or another coin is hit.

Leave an image and return to the original position.

Next turn is Blue's.

Feature idea # 4:

Modified script of the "orange" coin:

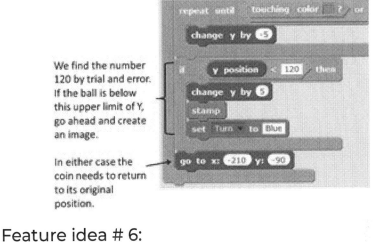

We find the number 120 by trial and error. If the ball is below this upper limit of Y, go ahead and create an image.

In either case the coin needs to return to its original position.

Feature idea # 6:

Script for base #2:

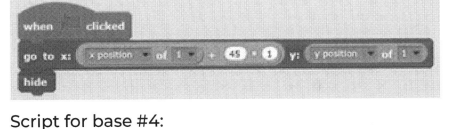

Script for base #4:

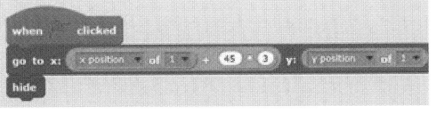

CONCLUSION

I want to thank you for taking the time to read this book! I certainly hope that you have found it informative and useful. The goal in this book was to keep things simple so that beginners can understand scratch and get started with using it, but hopefully, we've kept it interesting and fun as well.

Coding is a challenging and fun career, and since society is getting more dependent on computers and networks, the need for coders is only going to increase. Of course, even if your child is not going to be a coder, they can still benefit in many ways from learning some coding. First off, coding helps to train the mind to think carefully. Coding will help your child learn how to focus on and complete things that they have started. One lesson that all parents should strive for is making sure that children complete the projects that they start at scratch. This alone is a skill worth learning, even if they don't continue to code later.

Coding will also help children develop skills in logical thinking. You don't have to be a math whiz to do basic coding, but learning to code is going to improve the math skills of anyone who learns it and help them to think logically.

The best approach to use is to find simple tasks on the site, but tasks that are also interesting. One task that is good to try is one we touched on in the book. That is the animated letters. This is a fun task that children enjoy, and it lets them directly connect the commands they are giving the computer to the action that they see on the screen. The animation process can also involve several different methods, and so it also gives the children a chance to learn a lot about scratch, in a simple context.

There are many other good lessons to learn. However, if you are browsing around the MIT site, you are going to find that many of the projects posted on the site are quite sophisticated. Many of these have been developed by scratch fans in the general public. They can be instructive later, but they may not be suitable for beginners. The worst thing that can be done is intimidating a child by having them encounter codes that are complicated, and when they are just starting out, they may find that overwhelming. It will destroy the child's confidence. The site does provide many beginners tutorials. You can rely on those until the child has gained some experience. Then they can learn more complex programs that will take a longer time to figure out.

When guiding your children with scratch, it is important not to force them to do it. Not everyone is going to be inclined to do computer programming. If some children find it uninteresting, let them try something else. It is not going to be the end of the world if your child does not grow up to be a coder.

Again, thank you for reading my book. Please drop by Amazon and leave a thoughtful review, we'd love to hear how the book is helping you and your children!

Printed in Great Britain
by Amazon